FACILITATING BREAKTHROUGH

Facilitating Breakthrough

How to Remove Obstacles, Bridge Differences, and Move Forward Together

Adam Kahane

Foreword by Edgar H. Schein

A Reos Partners Publication

BK®

Berrett–Koehler Publishers, Inc.

BERRETT-KOEHLER PUBLISHERS, INC.
1333 Broadway, Suite 1000 Oakland, CA 94612-1921
Tel: (510) 817-2277   Fax: (510) 817-2278   www.bkconnection.com

ORDERING INFORMATION
Quantity sales. Special discounts are available on quantity purchases by corporations, associations, and others. For details, contact the "Special Sales Department" at the Berrett-Koehler address above.
Individual sales. Berrett-Koehler publications are available through most bookstores. They can also be ordered directly from Berrett-Koehler:
Tel: (800) 929-2929; Fax: (802) 864-7626; www.bkconnection.com.
Orders for college textbook / course adoption use. Please contact Berrett-Koehler: Tel: (800) 929-2929; Fax: (802) 864-7626.
Distributed to the U.S. trade and internationally by Penguin Random House Publisher Services.

Berrett-Koehler and the BK logo are registered trademarks of Berrett-Koehler Publishers, Inc.

PRINTED IN THE UNITED STATES OF AMERICA.

Berrett-Koehler books are printed on long-lasting acid-free paper. When it is available, we choose paper that has been manufactured by environmentally responsible processes. These may include using trees grown in sustainable forests, incorporating recycled paper, minimizing chlorine in bleaching, or recycling the energy produced at the paper mill.

Library of Congress Cataloging-in-Publication Data

Names: Kahane, Adam, author. | Schein, Edgar H., writer of foreword.

Title: Facilitating breakthrough : how to remove obstacles, bridge differences, and move forward together / Adam Kahane ; foreword by Edgar H. Schein.

Description: First edition. | Oakland, CA : Berrett-Koehler Publishers, Inc., [2021] | Includes bibliographical references and index.

Identifiers: LCCN 2021016168 | ISBN 9781523092048 (paperback) | ISBN 9781523092055 (adobe pdf) | ISBN 9781523092062 (epub)

Subjects: LCSH: Conflict management. | Problem solving. | Cooperation.

Classification: LCC HM1126 .K338 2021 | DDC 303.6/9—dc23

LC record available at https://lccn.loc.gov/2021016168

FIRST EDITION
26 27 28 25 24 23 22 21   10 9 8 7 6 5 4 3 2

Production manager: Susan Geraghty
Cover design: Daniel Tesser, Studio Carnelian
Interior design: Gopa & Ted2 Design
Composition: Westchester Publishing Services
Copyeditor: Michele D. Jones
Proofreader: Cathy Mallon
Indexer: Carolyn Thibault
Author photo: Dave Chan

To my teachers

Contents

Foreword by Edgar H. Schein

*T*he key to this book is the second word in its title: *breakthrough*. With powerful stories from around the world, Adam Kahane tells us how he and his colleagues have worked with groups, both within organizations and across larger social systems, that are stuck in complexity and conflict. This book provides us with profound insight into how transformative facilitation helps such groups get unstuck and move forward: to collaborate to make progress toward shared goals.

At the same time, this book makes a strong statement about the nature of those shared goals—learning to live together in a way that love, power, and justice enhance and support one another. We learn how challenging this facilitation can be. Even as we read about the variety of strategies and tactics that the facilitators use, we are always reminded that they are dealing not with solving simple problems but with helping address complex challenges.

Coaches, consultants, teachers, therapists, and other professional helpers have evolved many variants of facilitation for the myriad of situations in which individuals or groups get stuck and need help. What different forms of facilitation have in common is the need for a third party, and a process for creating a container, a defused context, and a cultural island within which the third parties can use their own behaviors and interventions to help the parties move forward.

There are also many kinds of theories of how to do this, and there are many kinds of group problems that the different facilitators work with, so it becomes important to identify what is different in Kahane's approach, and why that difference is important in today's complex, conflicted, and interdependent world.

What is different in this book?

First, the author's vast experience as the third party working with groups that have become seriously stuck is unique both in what he has accomplished and in his ability to tell the story in a way that enables others to understand and appreciate the importance of his particular approach to facilitation.

Second, the book shows that facilitating is not just the clever interventions introduced by the consultant at a group meeting, but can and often must be a multiyear process of one or more consultants partnering with stakeholders to build trust and openness, and then organizing safe places for the parties to face one another, get to know one another, and build enough trust to be able to move forward together. All this requires innovation, experimentation, and agility to identify and remove the barriers to transformation.

Third, the facilitation that is described here deals not only with groups stuck in product development or marketing problems but also with ones embedded in deep political and economic conflicts that have historical roots and, therefore, have created strong resistance to even getting together, much less trusting one another enough to allow a third party to get involved.

Fourth, Kahane's transformative facilitation is a great exemplar of bringing forward two aspects of Kurt Lewin's philosophy of foundational social change: working on important social issues where getting groups unstuck is essential, and doing so with a model of experiential learning in which teacher (facilitator) and student (client) creatively combine their roles as needed to get unstuck. This kind of work in the late 1940s initially grew out of the Human Relations Labs held in Bethel, Maine, and in the Tavistock Clinic in the UK, and was combined with the important work of futurists such as Don Michael.[1]

Many of the interventions that were launched in those one- or two-week labs evolved into multiyear projects within global organizations and communities. They all had in common what was then labeled "action research," in which intervention was almost always defined as a shared process between the client system and the third-party interveners. We now take experiential learning for granted and have forgotten not only how new this model is but also how much we need it more than ever in resolving deep conflicts. This book will be an important exemplar of applying aspects of experiential learning philosophy to our current global problems, especially the problem of multinational competition around the issue of what to do about the imminent danger of climate change to human survival.

The stories that Kahane tells us make us realize how much third-party intervention has evolved. In the transformative facilitation model described in this book, we see elements of what we learned in the research on group dynamics and in my process consultation, Senge's learning organization, Heifetz's adaptive leadership, the open systems emphasis and spirit of inquiry that launched experiential learning in the early labs and is again being reaffirmed in Bushe and Marshak's dialogic organization development, and most recently in Scharmer's Theory U.[2] This history of the field invites us to think of transformative facilitation as a far broader and deeper set of practices rather than a single formulaic facilitation method. What makes this book so powerful is that in a concise and beautifully presented model, Kahane brings all of this together.

The Kahane model moves us forward in a significant way from just describing a consultant's interactive skills in dealing with clients to offering an in-depth overview of facilitation as the creation and management of new social systems and cultural islands that enable conflicting parties to get unconflicted, using both formal and informal methods as needed. Kahane provides us with key concepts that build on traditional polarities yet also offers a creative, fluid conceptual model of how to think about intervention in a more dynamic manner. Most of us who have consulted or coached would not even begin to be able to figure out how to work in some of the situations Kahane describes, much less know how to create the containers that enable this work in the first place.

Perhaps most important, Kahane's stories and the conceptual model around which he organizes them lead us to confronting the deep value and motivational issues that so often lead to the conflicts in the first place: our failure to integrate the powerful forces of (1) our need to achieve, how we express the motive of power; (2) our need to collaborate and live together, how we express the motive of love; and (3) our need to do this fairly, to experience a sense of justice.

I encourage you to find out in this book what this very courageous transformative facilitator has done to bring power, love, and justice together in real-world examples.

> —*Edgar H. Schein, Professor Emeritus,*
> *MIT Sloan School of Management,*
> *and author of* Process Consultation Revisited,
> Helping, *and* Humble Inquiry
> *December 2020*

Preface

*M*oving forward together is becoming less straightforward.

In many contexts, people face increasing complexity and decreasing control. They need to work with more people from across more divides. This is true both within organizations and in larger social systems.

In such situations, the most straightforward and commonplace ways of advancing—some people telling others what to do, or everyone just doing what they want to do—aren't adequate.

What is a better way?

One better way is through facilitating: helping a group collaborate across their differences to create change. The word *facilitate* means "to make easier," and facilitation enables a group to work together more easily and effectively. But for diverse groups facing increasing complexity and decreasing control, the most common approaches to facilitating—bossy vertical directing from above and collegial horizontal accompanying from alongside— also aren't adequate. These common approaches often leave the participants frustrated and yearning for breakthrough.

This book describes an uncommon approach to facilitating such breakthrough: transformative facilitation. This approach focuses on removing the obstacles that stand in the way of people contributing and connecting equitably. More fundamentally, it focuses on removing the obstacles to love, power, and justice. It enables people to bring all of themselves to making a difference. It is a liberating way to make progress.

Transformative facilitation doesn't choose either the bossy vertical or the collegial horizontal approach: it cycles back and

forth between them—not in a straight line—employing five pairs
of outer moves and five inner shifts (summarized in table M.1 at
the end of the book). In doing this, it produces a third approach
that delivers better results than either the vertical or horizontal
one alone. Transformative facilitation is a structured and creative
way to help diverse groups remove obstacles, bridge differences,
and move forward together. Transformative facilitation enables
breakthrough.

This book is for anyone who wants to facilitate breakthrough,
be it as a leader, manager, consultant, coach, chairperson, organizer, mediator, stakeholder, or friend. A facilitator isn't only an
earnest, energetic professional in a windowless conference room
or in a window in a video conference. It isn't only someone who
runs training or strategic planning exercises. It isn't only a referee or timekeeper. It is anyone who helps people work together
to transform their situation: in person or online, as a professional
or amateur, in the role of team leader or team member, in an
organization or community, with a small alliance or large movement, during one meeting or over an extended process. A facilitator is anyone who supports groups to collaborate to create
change.

This book offers a broad and bold vision of the contribution
that facilitation can make to helping people move forward
together.

My understanding of transformative facilitation is based on my
firsthand experience. I have worked as a professional facilitator,
all around the world, for more than thirty years. I am a cofounder
of Reos Partners, an international social enterprise that helps
people in business, government, and civil society collaborate to
address their most important and intractable issues. I have facilitated hundreds of processes with everyday teams of colleagues
working to transform their organization's strategy or operations,
and with groups of people from across organizations—including
people who don't agree with or like or trust each other—working
to transform their whole sector or society. So I have had lots of

opportunities for trial and error and lots of opportunities for learning.

This book reports what I have learned from these experiences. Kurt Lewin, a pioneering researcher of group processes, said, "There is nothing as practical as a good theory."[1] This book offers a new general theory and practice of facilitation.

Introduction

"You Are Removing the Obstacles to the Expression of the Mystery!"

*T*ransformative facilitation is an unconventional and powerful approach to helping people collaborate to effect transformation. I had been facilitating for decades, but it was only in a workshop in Colombia in November 2017 that I grasped what is distinctive and important about this approach. This book was conceived at that workshop.

A BREAKTHROUGH WORKSHOP

In the sunny outdoor restaurant of a small country hotel, a former guerilla commander and a wealthy businesswoman greet each other by name. The organizer of the workshop tells them he is surprised that they know each other. The businesswoman explains: "We met when I brought him the money to ransom a man who had been kidnapped by his soldiers." The guerilla adds: "The reason we're at this meeting is so that no one will have to do such things again."

Transformative facilitation enables such breakthrough.

This workshop brought together a diverse group of leaders to talk about what they could do to contribute to transforming

1

their country. Seventeen months earlier, in June 2016, the government of Colombia and the FARC (the Spanish acronym for the Revolutionary Armed Forces of Colombia) movement had signed a treaty to end their fifty-two-year war, in which thousands had been kidnapped, hundreds of thousands killed, and millions displaced. In October 2016, President Juan Manuel Santos was awarded the Nobel Peace Prize in recognition of this long-struggled-for accomplishment. Santos appointed Francisco de Roux, the former head of the Jesuit order in Colombia and a renowned peacemaker, to be president of the Commission for the Clarification of Truth, Coexistence, and Non-Repetition, one of the bodies established to implement the treaty. After decades of being at one another's throats, Colombians were now trying, amid much turmoil and trepidation, to break through and work together to construct a better future. Our workshop was part of this effort.

In January 2017, in the troubled southwest of the country, two civic-minded leaders, Manuel José Carvajal, a businessman with connections to the elite, and Manuel Ramiro Muñoz, a professor with connections to the grass roots, decided to organize a project to contribute to rebuilding that region's society and economy. Their idea was to bring together leaders who were representative of all the region's stakeholders: everyone with a stake in the future of the region and therefore an interest in making it better.

Carvajal and I had worked together twenty years earlier, so he knew my work, and now he and Muñoz engaged Reos Partners to support them in facilitating this new project. We helped them identify and enroll forty influential people from different sectors— politicians from different parties, former guerilla commanders, businesspeople, nonprofit managers, community activists—who, if they could collaborate, could make a real difference in the region. We also helped them get started on a yearlong program of work for this group, first to discuss what could happen in the future—a set of possible scenarios—and then what the group would do to create a better future—a set of initiatives. (In the years that followed, this group continued to grow their membership and their impact on the region.)

In November 2017, the first workshop of this group took place over three days at the country hotel. I was delighted that Francisco de Roux showed up: I had met him before and found him lively and interesting. I asked him why he had taken time away from his important national responsibilities to participate in this local event, and he said he wanted to learn about how we were enabling collaboration across diversity.

On the morning of the first day of the workshop, the participants were tense. They had major political, ideological, economic, and cultural differences, and major disagreements about what had happened in the region and what needed to happen. Some of them were enemies. Many of them had strong prejudices. Most of them felt at risk in being there; one politician insisted that no photographs be taken because he didn't want it known that he was sitting down with his rivals. But all of them had showed up anyway, because they hoped that the effort could contribute to creating a better future.

Our facilitation team had organized the agenda of the first day as a structured series of exercises to enable the participants to get to know one another and to understand one another's perspectives on what was happening and what they could do about it. In the first activity, they sat in a circle and each of them took one minute, timed with a bell, to introduce themselves. The activities that followed were precise and varied. Some were conducted all together in plenary and others in different groups of two, four, or six persons. Participants shared and synthesized their thinking using sticky notes, flip-chart paper, or toy bricks. They came together in the meeting room, at the restaurant, or on walks around the hotel grounds. Our facilitation team supported these activities attentively: arranging the workshop space, explaining the exercises, helping everyone to participate.

By the end of this first, long day, the participants had begun to relax and to hope that they could do something worthwhile together. One of them said he had been amazed "to see the lion lie down with the lamb." Then, when we all got up to go to dinner, de Roux rushed up to me, overflowing with excitement. "Now I see what you are doing!" he said. "You are removing the obstacles to the expression of the mystery!"

I knew de Roux was telling me something that was important to him—in Catholic theology, "the mystery" refers to the incomprehensible and unknowable mystery of God—but I didn't understand what he thought this meant for what we had been doing in the workshop. Over dinner we talked for a long time and he patiently tried to give me a secular explanation: "Everything is a manifestation of the mystery. But you cannot predict or provoke or program it: it just emerges. Our key problem is that we obstruct this emergence, especially when our fears cause us to wall ourselves off."

I found this conversation fascinating but baffling. I said, "I am not aware that I am doing what you say I am doing." He shrugged and said, "Maybe that's for the best."

De Roux's cryptic comments intrigued me. I understood that the mystery is intrinsically, well, mysterious—not in the sense of a mystery that is solved at the end of an Agatha Christie novel, but in the sense of something that is important but cannot be seen or grasped. Maybe, I thought, it was some sort of felt but invisible force, like gravity, that, if we could remove the obstacles, would pull us forward—like a mountain stream that, if we could remove the boulders that have tumbled in and are blocking and dispersing the water, would run freely downhill in a strong, coherent flow.

THE PRACTICE OF REMOVING OBSTACLES

De Roux's observation enabled me to see my longtime work as a facilitator in a new light. Most facilitators, including me up to this point, talk about their work in terms of getting participants to do things. But now I realized that in fact most of the people

I work with want to or think they need to collaborate, in spite of or because of their differences. And when they succeed in doing so, they are overjoyed. The essence of what I am now calling transformative facilitation is therefore not getting participants to work together but helping them remove the obstacles to doing so. You can't push a stream to flow, but if you remove the blockages, it will flow by itself. This realization transformed my understanding of facilitation.

What I found particularly intriguing in de Roux's observation was not his esoteric reference to the mystery but his pragmatic focus on removing obstacles to its expression. After dinner, I went back to my room and made a list of all of the actions our facilitation team had taken over the months leading up to this first workshop (our facilitation work had started as soon as we had begun the project and engaged the participants ten months earlier) and during that first day that I could now interpret as aimed at removing obstacles to these leaders collaborating to transform the region.

The approach we took in Colombia unblocked the three essential ingredients to moving forward together: contribution, connection, and equity.

Removing Obstacles to Contribution

Our facilitation team helped remove obstacles to *contribution* through creating opportunities for the participants to bring their diverse ideas, skills, and resources to bear on their collective task. One of the larger objectives of the project, beyond the workshops, was for the participants to support one another to act with greater effectiveness in their respective spheres of influence to create better futures.

All collaborations require contribution. The reason people collaborate is to harness the diverse contributions of diverse participants to achieve a common purpose. Most people want to contribute, but often there are institutional, political, economic, cultural, psychological, or physical structures that hinder or prevent them from doing so. The consequences of these obstacles are disempowerment and stifled creativity, energy, and growth. Transformative facilitation focuses on creating change in these domains—within the working space of the group, and possibly also beyond the group—that dismantles these structures, empowers participants, and thereby enables their contributions.

Removing Obstacles to Connection

In Colombia we removed obstacles to *connection* through creating opportunities within the project for the participants to get to know one another as persons and to work together as peers. This helped everyone see more of the whole regional system they were working with, including how it was being exemplified in the interactions within the group itself. One of the larger objectives of the project was to remove obstacles to connection among people throughout the region in order to stitch together the torn social fabric.

All collaborations require connection. Harnessing diversity requires inclusion and belonging. People's contributions can't be effective if people are not connected to one another, to the situation they are trying to address, and to their own thinking, feeling, and will. Most people want to connect, but there are structures that separate or exclude them. The consequences of these obstacles are estrangement and weakened communication, linkages, and relationships. Transformative facilitation focuses on dismantling these structures and thereby enabling connection.

Removing Obstacles to Equity

Finally, in Colombia we removed obstacles to *equity* through creating an egalitarian and respectful culture within the project: sitting in a circle without anyone having a superior position; giving everyone an equal opportunity to contribute in plenary and small-group sessions within workshops, and in activities between workshops; and making project decisions transparently and democratically. One of the larger objectives of the project was to create more equitable contribution and connection in the region. In this regard, the project provided a visible and influential example of a radically unconventional way of being and working together. Whereas in English we use the word *coexistence* to refer to such a peaceful situation, in Spanish they say *covivencia*, which has a more dynamic connotation of living together, as a couple does, with all of the attendant possibilities and tensions.

All collaborations require equity. Contribution and connection will be constrained if they are not equitable. Many people want contribution and connection to be inclusive and fair, but there are structures that give certain people more freedom, privilege, and power than others. As a consequence, some people have fewer opportunities to contribute and connect than others, and this impedes collaboration. Transformative facilitation focuses on dismantling these structures and thereby enabling equity.

A GENERAL THEORY AND PRACTICE OF
TRANSFORMATIVE FACILITATION

Transformative facilitation is a powerful approach to helping people collaborate to create change. I have told the story of facilitating the extraordinary process in Colombia because it illustrates this approach in bright colors. I have also told it because this is where I started to understand the essence of transformative facilitation: removing obstacles to contribution, connection, and equity.

In Colombia, my colleagues and I used this approach to help a group of leaders from across a region work together to address the challenges of that region. But transformative facilitation is powerful in many settings. At Reos we have used this approach to help all kinds of groups work together on all kinds of challenges all over the world: retail company managers in Mexico making a plan to enter new markets, university administrators in the US redesigning their emergency financial aid system, First Nations leaders in Canada finding new strategies for improving population health, community members in the Netherlands implementing low-carbon energy systems, businesspeople in Thailand creating systems to reduce corruption, and food companies, farmers, and nongovernmental organizations around the world creating more sustainable food supply chains.

Transformative facilitation is a widely applicable approach to helping people collaborate to create change.

WHERE TO USE TRANSFORMATIVE FACILITATION

Transformative facilitation can help people collaborate in many contexts:

- From across different backgrounds and different positions in different organizations, and so bringing different perspectives on, interests in, concerns about, and aspirations for the situation they are facing

- In small or large groups, teams, departments, committees, and task forces

- In all kinds of organizations, including companies, government agencies, educational and health care institutions, foundations, nonprofit organizations, and neighborhood and community associations, and in cross-organizational and multi-stakeholder alliances

- To deal with all kinds of challenges—internal organizational, management, and cultural in addition to external business, economic, political, social, and environmental ones

- At all scales—local, regional, national, and international

WHAT TRANSFORMATIVE FACILITATION IS AND IS NOT

Transformative facilitation is an unconventional approach to helping a group collaborate. It involves working through the purpose and objectives of the collaboration, who will participate in what roles, what process they will use, and what resources they will require, and reviewing and revising all these elements as the work unfolds.

Transformative facilitation is NOT

- Just the activity of standing at the front of a conference room or in the central window of a video conference. It includes all the activities involved in helping people move forward together, before, during, and in between meetings.

- A process that has a fixed duration. It can last for a few hours or a few years.

- A recipe. It is a way of working with groups and of discovering, one step at a time, what needs to be done.

- A specific methodology. It is an approach that can be used with any collaborative change methodology.

- A way of getting or pushing a group to advance. It is a way to remove the obstacles to their advancing on their own.

- An approach that I invented. It is an approach that many excellent facilitators use, in part and implicitly, which in this book I map in full and explicitly.

WHO CAN FACILITATE TRANSFORMATIVE FACILITATION

To emphasize the basics: transformative facilitation is facilitated by a facilitator. The role of a facilitator—or, more usually, a team of several facilitators dividing different parts of this role among them—is to strategize, organize, design, direct, coordinate, document, coach, and otherwise support the work of the group of people who are collaborating.

In general, a facilitator supports the group through focusing on and taking responsibility for the *process* the group is using, so that the group itself can focus on and take responsibility for the *content* of the work. The key point is that the group decides what they want to do and the facilitator supports them to do this. But this division of responsibilities is not always clear-cut: often the group needs to weigh in on the process, and sometimes the facilitator is involved and so has a relevant perspective on the content.

The role of the facilitator can be played by anyone who is willing and able, from time to time or on an ongoing basis, to help people collaborate to create change. A facilitator can be

- A professional or an amateur

- Someone who is given this role or who takes it

- A leader, manager, staff member, volunteer, organizer, chairperson, consultant, coach, mediator, or friend

- Someone who has a stake in the work at hand or is impartial

- A member of the group that is collaborating or someone from outside

How to use this book

Transformative facilitation is a particular approach to helping people collaborate. I have written this book to provide guidance for everyone involved in such efforts: facilitators, the collaborators they are facilitating, people who initiate or sponsor such collaborations, and facilitation students and teachers. Everyone who is involved in a collaboration will benefit from understanding the theory and practice of transformative facilitation.

This book builds on and goes beyond my previous ones. *Solving Tough Problems* and *Collaborating with the Enemy* explained how diverse groups, even ones that don't agree with or like or trust each other, can work together to address their most important challenges. This new book explains what facilitators need to do to support such groups: it is focused on the work of the facilitators rather than of the groups.

Transformative Scenario Planning explained one methodology for collaborating to shape the future. This book explains an unconventional and powerful foundational approach that facilitators can employ to help groups using any collaborative methodology, including not only transformative scenario planning but also, for example, appreciative inquiry, emergent strategy, Future Search, Open Space Technology, social laboratories, and Theory U.[1]

Power and Love explained how people who want to effect change need to employ not only power, the drive to self-realization, but also love, the drive to reunification. This book fills in a missing piece of this puzzle: it explains the need also to employ justice, the structure that enables power and love. Power, love, and justice are the fundamental drives that manifest as contribution, connection, and equity; facilitation that does not employ all three drives cannot enable transformation. This is the red thread that runs through this whole book, from its introduction in the Colombia story through to its full elaboration in the conclusion.

This book does not provide specific agendas, exercises, or checklists; many excellent texts already do this.[2] Instead it explains, through specific stories and the general principles derived from these, the five elements of the transformative approach to facilitation and the five pairs of outer moves and five inner shifts required of facilitators to be able to enact this approach. The stories I tell are of my own firsthand experiences of facilitating and the lessons I have learned from them. I have written about some of these experiences before in my books on other subjects; my focus here, however, is not on telling new stories but on eliciting new lessons.

The stories in this book are not presented in chronological order because the challenges of transformative facilitation do not arise linearly: they arise repeatedly and must be answered iteratively. Many of the stories (like the one from Colombia) are of experiences I had while I was facilitating a group for the first time, because these challenges all arise in all collaborations right from the outset and are often clearest when they first appear. My own learning has also not been linear; these challenges are not straightforward to work with, and I've had to learn many of the same lessons multiple times.

Part 1 of this book explains why transformative facilitation is necessary and powerful. Part 2 explains how to put this approach into practice. The conclusion explains the larger contribution that transformative facilitation can make to creating a better world.

Part 1

The Theory of Transformative Facilitation

*T*ransformative facilitation is a powerful way to help a group of people collaborate to transform the situation they are facing. For example, a company-wide team launches a game-changing product. A committee of school board administrators, teachers, parents, and students pushes for policies to increase racial equity. A task force from across a global nonprofit reworks the organization's operating norms in response to a series of management missteps. An alliance of health care organizations reorients its services to improve population health in its region. A group of politicians, businesspeople, and community leaders work together to reinvigorate their local economy.

My colleagues and I have employed transformative facilitation in all of these settings and others. We have learned that transformative facilitation is a powerful approach—not a conventional or straightforward one, but more effective at helping diverse groups achieve progress than these other approaches.

Transformative facilitation can be used in any group in any kind of organization, or across multiple organizations. It can be used to make progress on any kind of internal or external challenge the group is facing. It can be used by groups working all together in person, online, or asynchronously. And it can be used by anyone who wants to help the group do this, either from inside or outside the group.

Transformative facilitation is a way of supporting people to create change through collaborating with diverse others, rather than through forcing things to be the way only some people want them to be. It is an unconventional way in that it incorporates and goes beyond the two conventional ways that are opposite and in tension: the bossy vertical, directing from above to help the group as a whole achieve its objectives, and the collegial horizontal, accompanying from alongside to help each member of the group achieve their own objectives. It is also unconventional in that it focuses not on pushing the group to advance but on strategically and systematically removing the obstacles to its doing so.

Transformative facilitation is transformative in that it enables the group to break through the constraints of conventional ways of working and thereby to transform themselves and the situation they are dealing with.

The next five chapters explain how transformative facilitation works.

1

Facilitation Helps People Collaborate to Create Change

*F*acilitating is a way to help people move forward together that harnesses contribution, connection, and equity. There are, of course, other ways to help people move forward together. These range from fervently hoping to vigorously forcing, and many ways in between: encouraging, inspiring, rewarding, cajoling, manipulating, imposing. These other ways are sometimes effective.

Facilitating is necessary, however, when two conditions are met.

THE NEED FOR FACILITATION

Facilitation is necessary when people both want to create change and want to collaborate to do so. When these two conditions are met, these people have energy to work together, and the facilitator doesn't need to provide the energy to *get* them to move forward. The facilitator only needs to *support* them to use their own energy to move forward.

People Want to Create Change

The first condition is that people want to create change—in their team, in their organization, or in the world beyond their organization. This means that the situation they find themselves in is not the way they want it to be; they think that something is going wrong or could be going better. If this condition is not met—if people think that things are fine just as they are—then they can just carry on doing what they are doing, and facilitation is not necessary or effective. I once facilitated a group of civic leaders in Canada who were concerned about national political divisions, but when what they were coming to understand implied that they had to make some tough changes, the people for whom the status quo was working well enough lost energy for the project. A facilitated change process won't go far if the participants don't want their situation to change.

Sometimes the way people see their situation is that they simply have a problem, maybe easy or maybe difficult, that they need to solve. One example might be a project that is behind schedule and needs to be sped up. Other times they see themselves as facing a problematic situation: a situation that different people see as problematic from different perspectives and for different reasons, which they can work with and through but cannot neatly solve once and for all. An example might be a high death rate from opioids. In either case, however, this first condition is met if people face a challenge that they want to address.

People Want to Collaborate

The second condition is that people want to collaborate to address this challenge. This means that they don't think they can (or they prefer not to) address this challenge on their own or by forcing others to come along. If this condition is not met—if people prefer to act unilaterally—then facilitation is not necessary or effective. I have been involved in trying to organize several collaborations that didn't get off the ground because many of the people involved in the situation thought that they could be more successful at creating the change they wanted by acting on their own or just with their immediate colleagues, either because they were powerful or because they valued their autonomy. A facilitated change process won't start or won't go far if the necessary participants aren't willing to work together.

Sometime collaborating is easy and fun, when the people involved look at things the same way and like and trust one another. This might be the case in a team of close colleagues. But often the people who need to collaborate to be able to address a given challenge have different positions, perspectives, and sources of power (these differences are one reason many situations are problematic rather than simply problems), and sometimes these others include people they don't agree with or like or trust. An example might be an alliance of business or political rivals. In either case, however, this second condition is met if people think they need to work together with diverse others.

FACILITATION IN ORGANIZATIONS

Facilitation is often necessary in organizations because these two conditions are often met: people in the organization want to create change, and they want to collaborate with their colleagues to do so. This is true in organizations of all types: small and large companies, educational and health care institutions, governmental and intergovernmental agencies, foundations, nonprofits, community associations, and others. So people in these organizations often need facilitation and facilitators.

I first started facilitating when I was an employee in the global planning department of Shell, the multinational energy company. Shell had oil, gas, coal, chemicals, and metals businesses in more than one hundred countries. Throughout the company, management teams faced problematic situations of all kinds, related to market conditions, government and community relations, human resources development, and other everyday and exceptional challenges. The culture of the company encouraged participation and debate, so these teams often held facilitated team meetings, workshops, and retreats to work out how to deal with these challenges. Usually the facilitators of these exercises were from within the same department, sometimes from another part of the company (such as the global planning department), and occasionally from universities or consulting companies.

An organization exists to bring people together to address the challenges that arise in achieving a particular mission. In many organizations, the default way of addressing such challenges is through *forcing*: the bosses decide what needs to happen and make that happen, whether or not their subordinates agree. Often people choose *adapting*: going along with things they don't agree with because they don't think they can change these things. Other times people choose *exiting*: quitting their jobs because they don't like what's happening, don't think they can change it, and aren't willing to live with it. But, in addition to these three unilateral options, people often also choose the multilateral option: *collaborating* within and across organizational teams and departments to get things done cooperatively and creatively. Facilitation is necessary when people want to collaborate to create change.

Facilitation can take many forms. People can collaborate in a one-hour meeting or a multiday workshop, in person or on a video conference, all together or with different individuals or groups doing different activities at different times in different places. Whatever the form, the role of the facilitator is to help the group connect and contribute more equitably, so as to create change more effectively.

At Reos, my colleagues and I facilitate in many kinds of organizations, always in partnership with managers and staff from within that organization. We helped managers in a chemicals company change their strategy to deal with new government regulations. We helped the staff of a hospital system reduce overcrowding. We helped the leaders of a foundation reprioritize their global activities in light of geopolitical shifts. In all these cases, facilitation was necessary because a diverse group faced a problematic situation and wanted to collaborate to change it.

FACILITATION BEYOND ORGANIZATIONS

Facilitation is often also necessary beyond organizations: in larger sectors, communities, and societies, which include multiple organizations of multiple types.

My first experience of facilitating in these settings was when I was still a Shell employee and was invited to facilitate a team of politicians, businesspeople, trade unionists, community activists, and academics in South Africa who wanted to use the Shell scenario planning methodology to think through the transition from apartheid to democracy. (This was the Mont Fleur scenario exercise, which I discuss in chapter 6.) South Africans have a rich history of employing different kinds of facilitation, in contexts ranging from traditional *lekgotlas* (a Sesotho word for village assemblies) to mass political movements, high-stakes union–management negotiations, and corporate *bosberaads* (an Afrikaans word for meetings held in the bush or on a game farm). I learned a lot of what I know about facilitation from South Africans.

Facilitating beyond organizations is less straightforward than within organizations because participants across larger social systems are more diverse and see their situations as problematic in more different ways. Such situations by definition include multiple centers of power, so more people need to participate to be able to effect change, and the participants often aren't sure they are willing or able to collaborate. In such cross-organizational contexts, facilitators need to do more work to organize the structures for collaboration than they do within a single organization. At the same time, because cross-organizational collaborations help people work together who have rarely or never had the opportunity to do so, the potential for breakthrough is also greater.

In the cross-organization project we facilitated in Colombia, the project organizers wanted to effect change in the region and thought that to do this they would need the active participation of leaders from across the region's whole social-political-economic-cultural system. This is why they involved politicians, former guerillas, businesspeople, philanthropists, researchers, activists, peasants, and Black and Indigenous leaders. The participants occupied many different positions in the system and so together had a greater capacity to understand and influence it than any of them alone.

The participants all thought that the situation in the region was problematic, but from many different perspectives. Some were primarily concerned about the difficulties in implementing the peace accords, and others about community safety, infrastructure, corruption, land ownership, Indigenous rights, or poverty. It therefore took days for the participants just to understand how others saw the situation, and more time to agree on what was most important and what needed to be done.

Some of these participants had tried dealing with what had been happening in the region through forcing: by using their authority or money or guns. Many of the others had thought they couldn't change what had been happening, so had tried adapting to get on with their lives as best they could. A few of them had tried exiting or emigrating from the country altogether. The people who had chosen to come to the workshop thought that the three unilateral options might be inadequate, so they came to try out this fourth, multilateral, collaborating option.

At Reos, my colleagues and I have facilitated many such diverse groups in cross-organizational systems. We helped a group of businesspeople, union leaders, and government regulators implement ways to make the apparel industry more environmentally and socially sustainable. We helped an international group of entrepreneurs find ways to make insurance more accessible. We helped a group of CEOs of environmental organizations collaborate to fight against climate change. In all of these cases, facilitation was useful and necessary because the people involved faced a problematic situation and wanted to collaborate to change it.

Groups of people, in and beyond organizations, often need facilitation. To be able to move forward together, one or several people, within or outside these organizations, need to act as facilitators. The next chapter explains how facilitators typically perform this role.

2

Conventional Vertical and Horizontal Facilitation Both Constrain Collaboration

A facilitator helps a group, and the tension starts right there. The word *group* is both a singular and plural noun, and the task of the facilitator is to help both the singular group as a whole and the plural members of the group. This is the core tension underlying all facilitation.

Some facilitators deal with this tension by focusing primarily on the first part of this task: helping the group as a whole address the problematic situation that has motivated their collaboration. Other facilitators focus primarily on the second part: helping the diverse individual members of the group address the diverse aspects of the situation that they find problematic.

These two approaches, the vertical and the horizontal, are the most common and conventional approaches to facilitation. Both have their proponents and methodologies. Both can help a group collaborate to create change. But both also have limits and risks.

VERTICAL FACILITATION

The most common approach to facilitation is vertical facilitation.

Table 2.1: Two Conventional Approaches to Facilitation

	VERTICAL FACILITATION	HORIZONTAL FACILITATION
Primary focus	The good of the singular whole of the group	The good of each part of (participant in) the group
Strategy for moving forward together	Pushing from the top down (compelling)	Pushing from the bottom up (asserting)
	Relying on expertise and authority	Relying on each participant choosing what they will do
Organizing principle	Hierarchy of the higher over the lower and the larger over the smaller	Equality
Upsides	Coordination and cohesion	Autonomy and variety
Downsides	Rigidity and domination	Fragmentation and gridlock

Definition

Vertical facilitation focuses on the singular whole of the collaboration: the one united team, the one definition of the problem, the one best solution, the one optimum plan, and, ultimately, the one superior leader who can decide what the group will do. (For a summary of the characteristics of vertical and horizontal facilitation, see table 2.1.)

It assumes that expertise and authority—of the more knowledgeable or senior participants and of the facilitator—are required to make progress on problematic situations.

It is vertical in that it is based on this hierarchy of the larger over the smaller and the higher over the lower.

Strategy

The strategy of vertical facilitation to help people move forward together is to push them to do so from the top down. It assumes that a situation will change only if the leaders make it change.

Here are two examples of vertical facilitation:

- A corporate planning exercise, where all the units in the organization are required to articulate how, in conjunction with other units, they will contribute to the mission and bottom line of the organization

- A policy formation process, through which multiple experts and authorities must work together to formulate a single common proposal

Context

My formative professional experiences all emphasized the vertical: the importance of focusing on the good of the singular whole and of employing expertise and authority to make progress on achieving that good. When I was in graduate school, my research in energy policy dealt with governmental actions to produce optimal economic and environmental solutions to energy problems. My first jobs were in the corporate planning departments of Pacific Gas & Electric and of Shell, where I coordinated efforts to create company-wide strategies and plans. And when I started to work as an independent consultant, most of my clients were hierarchical companies and government departments, where I facilitated dozens of workshops aimed at reaching and implementing agreements as to how to address the various challenges these organizations were facing. I was used to being in privileged, high-rank positions, so I understood and was comfortable working in these vertical systems.

Vertical facilitation is the most common approach to facilitation because verticality is the dominant organizing principle of most organizations and of other social systems. You know you're in a vertical system when you keep looking up to the boss to know what to do (the higher above the lower), and when fitting in and being a good team player or community member are of paramount importance (the larger above the smaller). When you're part of such a system, you sometimes have the feeling of being held down or boxed in, and find that you're silencing yourself or compromising on things that are important to you. In these ways, verticality constrains contribution, connection, and equity.

Vertical facilitation is the default approach in most organizations in most sectors in most parts of the world. Most people in positions of authority depend on and default to verticality because they believe that it is the only feasible way to produce forward collective action (and also to protect and advance their own interests). When they are involved in a collaboration to create change, they employ their authority to push for the contribution, connection, and equity that the work requires—although not necessarily more than is required.

Facilitating

Most facilitators default to vertical facilitation, especially facilitators who feel insecure or frightened. They focus on methodologies that get participants to accomplish the collective task, and worry about how to deal with the "difficult people" who resist the collective.

These facilitators see their primary job as pushing everyone to get them to contribute to the success of the collective endeavor. They urge the group to "trust the process," "focus on the good of the team," and "leave your own agendas at the door." But when they make these requests, the facilitator is ignoring the fact that every participant has their own interests—those related to their personal needs or those of their department or organization—that are only partly aligned with those of the group as a whole. There are only one or two persons—the facilitator themself and perhaps the boss of the group—for whom success in following the process and accomplishing the task of the group is identical with their own interests. Such requests are therefore disingenuous and manipulative.

Results

The upsides of vertical facilitation are coordination and cohesion. Vertical facilitation hammers out the agreements that the group needs so as to move forward together with unity. These are enormously valuable upsides.

But overemphasizing vertical facilitation also produces downsides: rigidity and domination. Pushing coordination and cohesion without leaving room for autonomy and variety results in the dominant members of the group forcing the subordinate members into straitjackets so that they feel unable to be themselves and say what they think. These downsides constrain contribution, connection, and equity.

In some contexts, the vertical might be good enough—but it has limits.

HORIZONTAL FACILITATION

The second most common approach to facilitation is the opposite of vertical facilitation: horizontal facilitation.

Definition

Horizontal facilitation focuses on the multiple parts of the collaboration: the positions and interests of the individual members of the group (who often don't see themselves as a team), their different understandings of the problematic situation, multiple possible solutions and ways forward, and, ultimately, their separate decisions about what they will do.

It assumes that in order to make progress on problematic situations, each participant needs to choose for themself what they will do—that no one can or must exercise superior expertise or authority.

It is horizontal in that it rejects hierarchy as illegitimate and ineffective. It emphasizes equality.

Strategy

The strategy of horizontal facilitation is to help people move forward together by encouraging them to push from the bottom up. It assumes that a situation will change only when people choose to stand up and advocate for taking action that creates change— and then to take those necessary actions. These participants must push for contribution, connection, and equity. The focus of the facilitator is therefore on promoting the rights, safety, and good of every participant.

Here are some examples of horizontal facilitation:

- A team training in which the strategy for creating collective change focuses on the learning and growth of each participant

- A community dialogue, where the emphasis is on each member having an equal right to provide their input on the matter at hand and to draw their own conclusions as to what to do about it

- A multi-stakeholder network or alliance, where each member is autonomous and must choose what they will do, together with and apart from the other members

- A negotiation, where the primary criterion for success is that every party is satisfied

Context

My largest area of work at Reos has been facilitating processes (such as the one in Colombia) that bring together leaders from different parts of a social system to make progress on a problematic situation that they all have a stake in and are concerned about. Such collaborations usually default to horizontality because the participants are not part of a single organizational hierarchy, and they value and guard their autonomy. I have observed similar dynamics in facilitating groups of academics and of activists, where in both cases participants value and guard their freedom. Such horizontal efforts may produce interesting ideas and initiatives by individual participants, but often result in limited collective action or systemic change.

Horizontal facilitation is a common approach in organizations and other social systems where horizontality is the dominant organizing principle. You know you're in such a system when you are encouraged and expected to do your own thing and to look after yourself: when autonomy and freedom are core values. When you're in such a system, you sometimes have the feeling of being alone and separated from others, and find that it's difficult to work with others to get things done or to change the way things are. In these ways, horizontality constrains contribution, connection, and equity.

Facilitating

Many facilitators recognize the oppressive downsides of vertical facilitation and therefore, in opposition, default to horizontal facilitation. They see their primary job as leveling the playing field to make sure that everyone gets an equitable opportunity to contribute to and benefit from the collaboration. Such equity, however, requires more than arranging the chairs of the group in a circle; it requires attending not only to the structures and dynamics inside the collaboration but also to those outside it.

Results

The positive contribution of horizontal facilitation is the encouragement of plural self-motivated actions to achieve a shared purpose. This approach encourages autonomy and variety: every participant being themself fully and expressing themself freely. These are enormously valuable upsides.

But overemphasizing horizontal facilitation also produces downsides: fragmentation and gridlock. Pushing autonomy and variety without leaving room for coordination and cohesion results in everyone doing their own thing and going their own way, feeling unable to work closely with others. These downsides diffuse and therefore constrain contribution, connection, and equity.

In some contexts, the horizontal might be good enough—but it has limits.

———

Both of the conventional approaches to facilitation, the vertical and the horizontal, produce valuable upsides and can work well for a while. But both also, when overemphasized or pursued on their own for too long, produce downsides. These downsides inevitably reduce and place at risk the effectiveness of these approaches to helping people move forward together. The next chapter proposes an unconventional approach to dealing with this tension.

3

Unconventional Transformative
Facilitation Breaks through
Constraints

*M*ost facilitators choose to employ either vertical facilitation or its polar opposite, horizontal facilitation. They argue that the approach they have chosen is more suitable and better than the other one. But when they make this choice, they inadvertently and inevitably constrain the potential of the collaborations they are facilitating, because neither of these conventional choices can create transformative change.

The vertical and horizontal approaches are, however, more than just opposite poles: they are complementary. This means that each of these approaches is incomplete without the other approach and that the downsides of each can be mitigated only through including the other.[1] Facilitation can therefore only be transformative—can only break through the constraints of the vertical and horizontal—if the facilitator chooses to employ both approaches. This is the more powerful, unconventional choice.

THE FACILITATOR CYCLES BETWEEN THE
VERTICAL AND HORIZONTAL

The facilitator chooses both the vertical and horizontal poles the same way we all choose both inhaling and exhaling. Nobody ever argues about whether it is better to inhale or exhale. We cannot choose between them: if we only inhaled, we would die of too much carbon dioxide, and if we only exhaled, we would die of too little oxygen. Instead, we must do both, not at the same time but alternately. First we inhale to get oxygen into our blood; then, when our cells convert oxygen to carbon dioxide and the carbon dioxide builds up in our blood, we exhale to let the carbon dioxide out; then, when the oxygen in our blood falls too low, we inhale; and so on. This involuntary physiological feedback system maintains the necessary alternation between inhaling and exhaling and enables us to live rather than die. The crucial point about this rhythm is that inhaling and exhaling must each fall only partway into the downside before the body shifts to the opposite upside: if it fell all the way, the result would be death.

Transformative facilitation works the same way. Vertical and horizontal facilitation both have upsides and downsides (see figure 3.1). When excessive verticality starts to get the group stuck in rigidity and domination, the facilitator emphasizes plurality to move toward horizontal autonomy and variety. When excessive horizontality starts to get the group stuck in fragmentation and gridlock, the facilitator emphasizes unity to move toward vertical coordination and coherence. This attentive series of choices maintains the necessary alternation between the vertical and horizontal approaches (the infinity sign or lemniscate). The crucial point about this rhythm is that the facilitator must notice when their vertical or horizontal facilitation is falling partway into the downsides, and at this point they must shift to the opposite upside: if the facilitation fell all the way, the result would be polarization and stuckness (the downward spiral). Cycling back and forth between vertical and horizontal facilitation produces facilitation that enables a group to move forward together (the upward spiral). This approach does not move in a straight line and is never straightforward.

This third approach to facilitation is transformative (see table 3.1). It is not simply a mixture of or compromise between

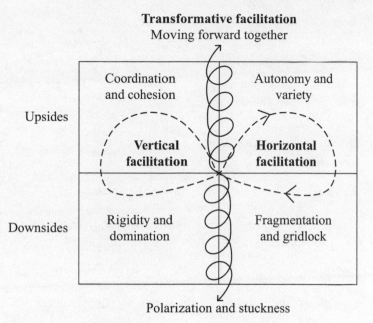

Transformative facilitation
Moving forward together

	Coordination and cohesion		Autonomy and variety
Upsides	**Vertical facilitation**		**Horizontal facilitation**
Downsides	Rigidity and domination		Fragmentation and gridlock

Polarization and stuckness

Figure 3.1: The cycle of transformative facilitation

vertical and horizontal facilitation: it includes and transcends these two and transforms them into an approach that is fundamentally different. The constraints of vertical and horizontal facilitation mean that both of these approaches can only create limited change, but transformative facilitation removes these constraints by removing the obstacles to moving forward together (that is, by transforming the group). Only transformative facilitation can create breakthrough transformative change.

Cycling removes obstacles

Both vertical and horizontal facilitation focus on pushing through the structural obstacles to moving forward together, but transformative facilitation focuses on *removing* these obstacles. This approach to creating change has a long pedigree: in the 1940s, pioneering organizational development researcher Kurt Lewin

Table 3.1: Three Approaches to Facilitation

	VERTICAL FACILITATION	TRANSFORMATIVE FACILITATION	HORIZONTAL FACILITATION
Primary focus	The good of the singular whole of the group	The good of the system of wholes and parts	The good of each part of (participant in) the group
Strategy for moving forward together	Pushing from the top down (compelling)	Removing structural obstacles (enabling)	Pushing from the bottom up (asserting)
	Relying on a hierarchy of expertise and authority	Cycling back and forth between the vertical and horizontal	Relying on each partici-pant choosing what they will do
Organizing principle	Hierarchy of the higher over the lower and the larger over the smaller	Equitable hierarchy	Equality
Upsides	Coordination and cohesion	More of the best of the vertical and horizontal	Autonomy and variety
Downsides	Rigidity and domination	Less of the worst of the vertical and horizontal	Fragmentation and gridlock

posited that removing obstacles is more effective than increasing pressure:

> Instead of simply applying pressure or forcing a change, Lewin's research supports identifying and addressing restraining forces as a foundation for successful planned change: "In the first case [of applying pressure], the process . . . would be accomplished by a state of relatively high tension, [while] in the second case [of addressing restraining forces] by a state of relatively

low tension. Since increase of tension above a certain degree is likely to be paralleled by higher aggressiveness, higher emotionality, and lower constructiveness, it is clear that as a rule, the second method will be preferable to the [first]."[2]

In transformative facilitation, the facilitator makes both vertical and horizontal moves to remove structural obstacles to contribution, connection, and equity. The following are some examples of such structural changes:

> Setting up in-person and online working spaces to enable fluidity and creativity in who works with whom on what (through emphasizing flexibility and choice)

> Giving everyone an opportunity to collaborate with many different others (through working in multiple mixed small groups, along with informal breaks and meals and other ways to connect)

> Encouraging the rapid and participative generation and iteration of ideas (using physical and virtual flip charts and whiteboards, sticky notes, building blocks, and shared files).

In all these examples, the facilitator's vertical moves are setting up new structures, and their horizontal moves are inviting participants equitably to employ these structures to contribute and connect all of their diverse concerns, ideas, commitments, gifts, and energies.

Cycling back and forth between the vertical and horizontal is like rocking back and forth a boulder that is blocking a stream, in order to dislodge it and enable the stream to run with greater coherence and flow. The facilitator employs five vertical and five horizontal moves to help a group move forward together with greater coherence and flow. These moves are introduced in chapter 4, explained in chapters 6–10, and summarized in

A Map of Transformative Facilitation (table M.1) at the end of the book.

When a facilitator removes obstacles that block contribution, connection, and equity, they are performing a radical act. In many contexts, this act challenges the status quo, and participants who prefer the status quo will push back. To be successful in helping participants deal with such problematic situations, the facilitator needs to be aware of and respond strategically to dynamics that try to keep things the way they are. For example, dominant participants may try to impose their wishes on the group (through talking over others or using their authority to shape the group's agenda or priorities), and in these cases the facilitator will need to negotiate group rules (including rules for making decisions) to ensure adequate contribution, connection, and equity.

Removing obstacles can also be a simple act. For example, the round of one-minute introductions at the beginning of the first Colombia workshop helped unblock contribution by enabling the voice of every person to be heard. It helped unblock connection by enabling everyone to see and hear everyone else. And it helped unblock equity by using the circle of chairs, with no one at "the front" of the room, and the one-minute bell, with no one given extra time because of their rank. This precisely designed first session set the pattern for everything that followed in the project. Transformative facilitation consists of simple actions undertaken with strategic intentionality.

TRANSFORMATIVE FACILITATION ENABLES CHANGE IN ORGANIZATIONS

Early in my career as an independent consultant, my colleagues and I facilitated a two-year strategy project for a Fortune 50 logistics company. The company's established way of doing things was vertical: the CEO managed through giving forceful, detailed directives, which had produced the coordination and cohesion that enabled outstanding business success. But the COO thought that the company's situation was problematic in that globalization and digitization were changing the competitive landscape, and he wanted employees from across the organization to collaborate more horizontally to create innovative responses.

My team worked with the COO and his colleagues vertically to agree on a project scope, timeline, and process, and to charter a cross-level, cross-departmental team. The process we designed for the team was more horizontal, participative, and creative than they were used to. They immersed themselves in the changes in their market by spending time on the front line of the organization, going on learning journeys to leading organizations in other sectors, and constructing scenarios of possible futures. They participated in workshops that emphasized full participation by all team members and that included structured exercises to generate, develop, and test innovative options.

This transformative process enabled breakthrough by creating a space within which the company's culture of command and control, which assumed that the bosses knew best, was suspended. This enabled greater contribution by participants across different departments and from different levels in the hierarchy. The cross-departmental project team cut across the siloed organization, where lines of communication ran up and down rather than side to side, so the process enabled greater connection. And the company had a steep hierarchy of privilege, with senior people having much greater compensation and agency, so the process also enabled more equitable contribution and connection. Transformative facilitation enabled this team to come up with and implement a set of initiatives to launch new service offerings and to streamline company operations.

TRANSFORMATIVE FACILITATION ENABLES CHANGE BEYOND ORGANIZATIONS

In larger social systems that include multiple organizations of different types, the structures that encourage or constrain contribution, connection, and equity are larger and more complex than those within single organizations. Employing transformative facilitation in such systems therefore requires implementing strategic interventions to transform these structures, including through creating and growing new ones.

In our project in Colombia, for example, our first step was to convene the participants. The project initiators took many months to recruit leaders from all the region's economic, political, social, and ethnic groups, including both the elite and the marginalized. They asked other influential people to endorse the project to give it credibility and to give the participants formal and informal authorization. They found an organization to fund the project and another to donate the hotel space.

The collaboration needed to be properly organized. We designed the project to provide support to the participants over the course of their work up to and during the first workshop and for the year that was to follow. We assembled a facilitation team that included the Reos team, with our international experience in facilitating such cross-organizational processes, plus locals with experience and relationships in the region. This team spent two days to get to know one another and to work out how to approach our role as facilitators.

To be able to work together, the participants needed to create enough of a common language to be able to talk about the situation in the region and how they could change it. We conducted open-ended interviews with each of them, both to enroll them in the project and to hear their views on the key issues facing the region. We then compiled these views into a report containing a selection of their unattributed verbatim statements, which we distributed in advance of the first workshop. On the first morning of the workshop, each participant presented their perspective on the current reality of the region, along with a physical object they had brought (these included a stone, a book, a seed, and a machete), which produced fresh metaphorical images. They used toy bricks to build models of the social-political-economic-cultural system of the region in its larger context, enabling them to share and combine their different tacit understandings visibly and fluidly. They wrote and organized their ideas on sticky notes, helping create and iterate their composite understanding of the current reality. All of these methodologies created space for all of the participants, including minority and marginalized ones, to express themselves equally and openly, and helped make visible some of what had been invisible.

Most crucially, the participants needed to be willing and able to work together. To support them in connecting better with one another, we

> Agreed on a set of ground rules, especially about confidentiality, that helped them feel safer to make their contributions.

> Ate our meals together at long tables, which created a space for informal conversations.

> Invited them to go on walks in pairs, which enabled the development of personal connections across divides.

> Introduced a framework for open, nonjudgmental, empathetic listening, which they practiced in pairs; the final step in this exercise involved looking into their partner's eyes, and the unfamiliar and unexpected sense of connection in the room was palpable.

> Facilitated an hour during which the participants told personal stories about their lives, which enabled them to understand better why some of them had ended up on opposing paths.

And we did all of these unconventional activities in a structured yet playful sequence, inviting the participants to relax and open up to what could happen—the expression of the mystery.

In everything our Colombian facilitation team did, then, we systematically employed both our vertical expertise and authority and the horizontal choices of the participants to remove the obstacles to contribution, connection, and equity.

———

In transformative facilitation, the facilitator cycles back and forth between the vertical and horizontal to unblock contribution, connection, and equity, and thereby to enable the group to move forward together. The next chapter explains the specific moves the facilitator must make to accomplish this cycling.

4

The Facilitator Enables Breakthrough by Making Ten Moves

*A*cyclist pushes alternately on the left and right pedals to enable the bicycle to advance. Similarly, a facilitator makes alternating vertical and horizontal moves to enable the group to advance.

FIVE QUESTIONS ALL COLLABORATIONS MUST ADDRESS

Every collaboration is different because the particulars of the problematic situation, the participants, and the process are different. But in all collaborations, the participants and facilitators need to work through the same five basic how-to questions about how they will move forward together:

1. *How do we see our situation?* In other words, what is actually happening here, around, among, and within us? This question is about the reality (including the reality within the group) that the group is working together to address. If we can't understand our reality, we can't be effective in transforming it.

2. *How do we define success?* What outcomes are we trying to produce through our efforts? This question is about where we are trying to get to through our collaboration. If we don't know what our finish line is, we can't know whether we're making progress.

3. *How will we get from here to there?* What is our route from where we are to where we want to be? This question is about the way we will move forward—the approach, process, methodology, and steps.

4. *How do we decide who does what?* What is our approach to coordinating and aligning our efforts? This question is about how we will organize ourselves to collaborate across our differences (without necessarily relying on our usual roles and hierarchies).

5. *How do we understand our role?* What is our responsibility in this situation? This question is about how we each position ourselves vis-à-vis our situation and our collaborative effort to address it.

These questions all arise right from the beginning of every collaboration, but they usually don't get answered all at once or once and for all. Facilitators and participants need to deal with them repeatedly and iteratively over the duration of the collaboration, whether that is days or decades.

HOW VERTICAL AND HORIZONTAL FACILITATION ANSWER THE FIVE QUESTIONS

Vertical facilitation is common and seductive because it offers straightforward and familiar answers to these five questions. In this approach, both the participants and the facilitator typically give the following five confident, superior, controlling answers about the work they are doing:

1. "We have the right answer."

2. "We need to agree."

3. "We know the way."

4. "Our leaders decide."

5. "We must fix this."

In horizontal facilitation, by contrast, participants typically give the following five defiant, defensive, autonomous answers, and the facilitator supports this autonomy:

1. "We each have our own answer."

2. "We each need to keep moving."

3. "We will each find our way as we go."

4. "We each decide for ourselves."

5. "We must each get our own house in order."

HOW TRANSFORMATIVE FACILITATION ANSWERS THE FIVE QUESTIONS

The vertical and horizontal approaches answer the five collaboration questions in opposite ways. These pairs of statements constitute five polarities that are focused versions of the overall vertical–horizontal polarity. In transformative facilitation, the facilitator makes five sets of moves that help the participants cycle back and forth between each pair of poles. This is how the group obtains the best of both approaches, avoids the worst, and moves forward together.

How Do We See Our Situation?

The facilitator helps the participants work with this first question by helping them cycle between *advocating* and *inquiring* (see table 4.1). Often both the participants and the facilitator start off a collaboration with the confident vertical perspective, "We have the right answer." Each person thinks that "If only the others would agree with me, then the group would be able to move forward together more quickly and easily." But when the group takes this position too far or for too long and starts to get stuck in rigid certainty, the facilitator needs to help participants inquire to move toward horizontal plurality. When participants are pounding the table, certain that they have the right answer, the facilitator can encourage them to add "In my opinion" to the beginning of their sentence, and if that is insufficient, to try "In my humble opinion." These playful sentence stubs open the door to inquiry.

Then, when the participants take this horizontal "We each have our own answer" too far and for too long and start to get stuck in cacophony and indecision, the facilitator helps them advocate in order to move toward the clarity and decisiveness of vertical unity.

The facilitator moves back and forth between advocating and inquiring about what is happening within the group and what the participants need to do about this; in doing so, the facilitator encourages the group to do the same in regard to what is going on in the problematic situation and what they need to do to address it. Through this cycling between advocating and inquiring, the group and the facilitator gradually and iteratively clarify their understanding of where they are and what this implies for what they need to do next.

How Do We Define Success?

The facilitator helps the participants work with the second question by helping them cycle between *concluding* and *advancing*. Often both the participants and the facilitator start off a collaboration with the vertical perspective, "We need to agree." But when they take this position too far or for too long and start to get stuck in this demand for a conclusion, the facilitator needs to help

Table 4.1: The Cycling Moves of Transformative Facilitation

	VERTICAL FACILITATION	TRANSFORMATIVE FACILITATION		HORIZONTAL FACILITATION
	The typical answer that, when taken too far, indicates that the group is getting stuck in the downside of the vertical	The counter-vailing move that shifts the group toward the upside of the horizontal	The counter-vailing move that shifts the group toward the upside of the vertical	The typical answer that, when taken too far, indicates that the group is getting stuck in the downside of the horizontal
Overall	"We must focus on the good of the whole."	Emphasizing plurality	Emphasizing unity	"We must focus on the good of each part."
1. How do we see our situation?	"We have the right answer."	Inquiring	Advocating	"We each have our own answer."
2. How do we define success?	"We need to agree."	Advancing	Concluding	"We each need to keep moving."
3. How do we get from here to there?	"We know the way."	Discovering	Mapping	"We will each find our way as we go."
4. How do we decide who does what?	"Our leaders decide."	Accompanying	Directing	"We each decide for ourselves."
5. How do we under-stand our role?	"We must fix this."	Standing inside	Standing outside	"We must each put our own house in order."

them keep moving. One of my most important learnings as a facilitator has been that, in order to move forward together, agreement is not required as often or on as many matters as most people think.

Then, when the participants start to get stuck in the unfocused horizontal "We each just need to keep moving," the facilitator needs to help them pause to work out what they can agree to focus on.

In doing this cycling, the facilitator is working with a key tool of facilitation: the pace and timing of the process—when the group needs to slow down or pause to reach an agreement or conclusion, when it needs to keep advancing even with no or only partial agreement, and when it needs to declare that the collaboration must end. Through this cycling between concluding and advancing, the group and the facilitator gradually and iteratively clarify their understanding of where they want to get to.

How Will We Get from Here to There?

The facilitator helps the participants work with the third question by helping them cycle between *mapping* and *discovering*. Often both the participants and the facilitator start off a collaboration with the assured vertical perspective, "We know the way." But when they take this position too far or for too long and start to get stubbornly stuck, the facilitator needs to help participants experiment to test their understanding and to discover new options.

Later, when the participants start to get stuck in the horizontal "We will each just find our way as we go," the facilitator helps them map out a common way forward.

Sometimes the facilitator needs to persist with the planned process for the work of the group and the group needs to persist with its planned course of action to address the problematic situation. Sometimes they both need to pivot to deal with what is actually happening, which is different from what they had planned.

Through this cycling between mapping and discovering, the group and the facilitator gradually and iteratively clarify their way forward.

How Do We Decide Who Does What?

The facilitator helps the participants work with the fourth question by helping them cycle between *directing* (like the director of an orchestra or band) and *accompanying* (like an accompanist playing piano or drums). Often both the participants and the facilitator start off a collaboration with the unambiguous vertical perspective, "Our leaders decide." But when they take this position too far or for too long and start to get stuck in ineffective bossiness, the facilitator needs to help all participants take responsibility for their own actions.

Then, when the participants start to get stuck in the misaligned horizontal "We each need to decide for ourselves," the facilitator helps them align their actions.

Sometimes the facilitator needs to direct from the front of the group, and the group needs to be directive in addressing the problematic situation. Sometimes the facilitator needs to accompany from alongside the group, and the group needs to do the same from alongside the situation. Through this cycling between directing and accompanying, the group and the facilitator gradually and iteratively clarify how they are coordinating their work.

How Do We Understand Our Role?

The facilitator helps the participants work with this last question by helping them cycle between *standing outside* the problematic situation and *standing inside* it. Often both the participants and the facilitator start off a collaboration with the objective vertical perspective, "We must fix this." But when they take this position too far or for too long and start to get stuck in cold remoteness, the facilitator needs to help participants consider how they are part of the problem and therefore have the leverage to be part of the solution.

Then, when the participants start to get stuck in the self-centered and myopic horizontal "We must each put our own house in order," the facilitator helps them stand outside the situation to get a clearer, more nonpartisan and neutral perspective on what is happening.

Sometimes the facilitator also needs to stand outside to get a clearer perspective on what is happening and sometimes to stand inside it to recognize the ways in which they are also part of the problem and therefore have the leverage to be part of the solution. Through this cycling between standing outside and inside, the group and the facilitator gradually and iteratively clarify their roles and responsibilities.

Every group that is collaborating needs to work through the five basic questions, not just once at the beginning of the collaboration, but multiple times, iteratively, as the collaboration unfolds. The facilitator therefore needs to make the ten moves over and over as they are needed. The next chapter explains how the facilitator can know what move to make next.

5

The Facilitator Knows What Move to Make Next by Paying Attention

*T*ransformative facilitation involves making just ten moves. Facilitators need to make these moves, however, not in any straightforward or predefined order or rhythm, but as and when each move is needed, moment by moment. To do this effectively, facilitators need to pay attention to what is going on in and around the group and in themselves.

THE FACILITATOR ENABLES FORWARD MOVEMENT THROUGH CYCLING

The facilitator cycles back and forth among the five pairs of moves. At some times and in some contexts, the facilitator gives more weight to one of the pairs or to another, or more weight to a vertical move or to a horizontal one. For example, when the group is trying to understand what is happening among themselves and how this relates to what is happening in their larger situation (the first question), the facilitator can encourage them to see more by toggling between standing outside and inside (the fifth question). Or when the group is pausing to come to a conclusion (the second question), the facilitator can encourage them to focus on how the group makes decisions (the fourth question). Or, in a strongly vertical organizational culture, the facilitator may need to return often, reassuringly, to the vertical pole.

There is, however, no stable middle ground or static balance among these moves. As if they were riding a bicycle, the facilitator needs to keep alternating to establish a dynamic balance and to help the group move forward.

A beginner facilitator can get severely off balance and must then shift consciously and wrenchingly to rebalance. A master gets only slightly off balance and shifts unconsciously and fluidly. Even after three decades, I am only partway along this learning curve, and many of the stories in this book are of times I got off balance and how I rebalanced.

TRANSFORMATIVE FACILITATION INVOLVES PLAYING BOTH AN OUTER AND AN INNER GAME

Sports psychologist Tim Gallwey says, "In every human endeavor there are two arenas of engagement: the outer and the inner. The outer game is played on an external arena to overcome external obstacles to reach an external goal. The inner game takes place within the mind of the player."[1]

In the outer game of transformative facilitation, the facilitator makes the ten moves. In the inner game of transformative facilitation, the facilitator makes five attentional shifts within themself. These shifts enable the facilitator to know, at each moment, what move they need to make.

As the facilitator works with each of the five collaboration questions, they need to pay attention and shift in a specific way:

1. To cycle between advocating and inquiring, the facilitator needs to *open up*: to pay attention to what is happening and what is needed in the situation and in the group. (This first shift is foundational for the four others.)

2. To cycle between concluding and advancing, the facilitator needs to *discern*: to pay attention to when the group needs to slow down to agree, when to keep moving forward without or with only partial agreement, and when to stop and end.

3. To cycle between mapping and discovering, the facilitator needs to *adapt*: to pay attention to when to persist in following a planned route and when to pivot to try a new one.

4. To cycle between directing and accompanying, the facilitator needs to *serve*: to pay attention to when the group needs firm instruction and when it needs relaxed support.

5. To cycle between standing outside and standing inside, the facilitator needs to *partner*: to pay attention to when to focus on being apart from the group and the situation and when to focus on being part of it.

PAYING ATTENTION REQUIRES DEALING WITH DISTRACTION

Paying attention in these five ways is partly rational and partly intuitive. For example, when I am opening, I am listening to and analyzing the words participants are using, and also responding to subtle shifts in their visible gestures or invisible energies. When I am facilitating, I am not only or always listening to what people are saying: I am using all my senses to grasp what is going on in the group and what I need to do.

Just before a workshop starts, the facilitation teams I am part of always meet to "check in": to begin our work together by noticing and sharing where each of us is coming from and in this way to become fully present. On these occasions, I often find myself saying, "I am ready: I have finished off the other things I needed to do and am now fully here." I focus so diligently on finishing off those other things (tasks for other projects, personal matters, detailed preparations) because I know that while I am facilitating, it is crucial for me to pay attention without distraction.

All facilitators, even if they are not directing the group at a given moment—if they are providing logistical support, taking notes, or preparing for the next activity—need to be paying attention. One way in which facilitation is more challenging now than it used to be (whether in person or, even more so, online) is that facilitators and participants are easily distracted from paying attention to what is going on in the group, habitually checking their phones or computers. The reminder I most often have to give to fellow facilitators is, "Please stop looking at your phone." Part of paying attention is paying attention to yourself, both to notice your distraction and, when undistracted, to use your whole self as an instrument of perception.

The attention of facilitators wanders from what is going on in the group not only because of external distractions but also because of internal ones. They get caught up in their own inner dynamics—ego, reaction, projection, insecurity, defensiveness, fear. This happens to me when I become irritated by someone in a workshop (usually because of an experience I had with someone else elsewhere) or when I am upset by something happening in a project (usually because I am worried about something that might happen in the future). In such situations, I need to remember to pay attention again to what is going on here and now, just as in a meditation practice where the instruction is to keep bringing your attention back to your breath. Many of the stories I tell in this book about times I failed in my facilitating were of times when my internal dynamics, especially fear, overwhelmed my capacity to remain relaxed and attentive. Fear blocks contribution, connection, and equity.

I am becoming more masterful in my facilitation inasmuch as I can recenter myself more quickly than I used to. Rather than being distracted for hours in a workshop, I can usually bring my attention back within minutes, and rather than being upset during a project for weeks, I can usually compose myself within days.

The inner practice for facilitators is not so much to avoid becoming distracted as to learn to pay attention again more quickly and easily. This practice enables the facilitator to more readily shift and move as the situation requires, and thereby to help the participants do the same.

Paying attention enables fluidity

Psychologist Mihaly Csikszentmihalyi uses the term *flow* to describe the state of "being completely involved in an activity for its own sake. The ego falls away. Time flies. Every action, movement, and thought follows inevitably from the previous one, like playing jazz. Your whole being is involved, and you're using your skills to the utmost."[2] When I am facilitating at my best, fully attentive to what is going on in the group, I am in flow. This state of being fully attentive is thrillingly effective.

Massachusetts Institute of Technology researcher Otto Scharmer uses the term *presencing* to describe this state of sensing and being present "to a future possibility that is seeking to emerge," and the term *absencing* to describe the opposite.[3] A facilitator needs to presence rather than absence in order to be able to notice what is arising in the group moment to moment, and to do this with relaxation, compassion, and equanimity. This is the quality of attention required for the facilitator to notice what is actually happening—even if it is different from what they expected or wanted, or is surprising, confusing, or upsetting—and hence to be able to move and shift appropriately.

The facilitator learns to pay attention by practicing

A facilitator employing transformative facilitation in a group is like a sailor sailing a small boat in a strong wind. The sailor can't control the wind and so mustn't waste energy being upset about what it is doing. The way to move a sailboat in the direction from which the wind is blowing is not to point the boat directly toward the wind: it is to tack back and forth at an angle of around 45 degrees from the direction of the wind, over and over. The sailor tacks by making fluid adjustments to the direction of the boat, the position of the sail, and where in the boat they are placing their body weight. An experienced sailor knows what move to make next by paying attention both rationally and intuitively to what is happening in and around the boat. One valuable tool for this is small pieces of yarn attached to the sail ("telltales") that indicate small changes in the direction of the wind relative to the boat. If the sailor fails to pay attention, the boat will not move forward—it might even capsize.

The core skill required of the facilitator is, similarly, to pay attention. An experienced facilitator knows what move to make next by paying attention both rationally and intuitively to what is going on within and among the members of the group and in its context. The facilitator watches the telltales of this—for example, the statements that typically indicate that a group is getting stuck in the downside of one pole and requires the facilitator to make the countervailing move toward the upside of the opposite one. If the facilitator fails to pay attention, the collaboration might not move forward—it might even capsize.

Transformative facilitation is not straightforward. It requires moving forward, not in a straight line, but back and forth between two opposite approaches. And it requires paying attention not only to what is outside and visible but also to what is inside and invisible.

Hillel was a rabbi who lived in Jerusalem twenty-one hundred years ago. There is a story about a student who once challenged Hillel to explain the single fundamental principle of Jewish practice while standing on one foot. Hillel did not (as another rabbi had) chase the student away, but instead replied: "That which is hateful to you do not do to another; that is the entire Torah, and the rest is its interpretation. Go study."[4]

Nobody has ever asked me to explain transformative facilitation while standing on one foot. But if anyone ever did, I would reply: "Pay attention; the rest is interpretation. Go practice." The next part of this book explains the practice of transformative facilitation.

Part 2

The Practice of Transformative Facilitation

A facilitator uses transformative facilitation to help a group collaborate to transform their situation. Extending the examples I gave at the beginning of part 1, an engineer directs a company-wide product launch team. Two administrators initiate a school board racial equity committee and engage an external consultant to support their process. A human resources manager and her staff organize a global nonprofit's culture change task force. A team from across several organizations coordinate the work of a population health alliance. Five concerned citizens convene a local economy rejuvenation group.

My colleagues and I have partnered with the local facilitators in all of these settings and others. We have learned that the core of the practice of transformative facilitation is helping a group work through the five basic collaboration questions listed at the beginning of chapter 4. A facilitator does this through making five pairs of outer moves and five inner shifts, as and when these are needed (as discussed in chapter 5 and illustrated in table M.1). In doing this, they transform their own actions and help the group transform their actions and thereby their situation.

In April 2020, while I was writing this book, I moved from an apartment in the city to a house in the country. My daily jogging habit changed accordingly: I used to run on a grid of signposted streets, and now my route was through a forest crisscrossed by unmarked trails. For weeks I kept getting lost (especially when I was distracted by thinking about my writing) until I learned to recognize the signs—a fallen tree, a clearing, a widening of the path—that showed me at each point which direction I needed to turn. I built up a map in my head.

Transformative facilitation is like running in this forest. To help a group find its way forward, the facilitator needs to pay attention, moment by moment, to the signs of what is going on in and around the group, to be able to know at each point what moves and shifts to make.

The next five chapters build up a map of the five collaboration questions that every group needs to work through, repeatedly and iteratively, in order to move forward together, and of the moves and shifts that the facilitator needs to make to help the group do so.

6

How Do We See Our Situation?
Advocating and Inquiring

*I*n transformative facilitation, a facilitator helps a group collaborate to transform their problematic situation. In doing so, the first basic question they need to work with, and return to over and over, is: How do we understand what is happening in our situation?

In vertical facilitation, participants answer questions about their situation by confidently *advocating*: "We have the right answer." The facilitator gives exactly this same answer to questions about the process. Disagreements about these answers are settled either through debate among the proponents of different answers (with one prevailing) or by the decree of the most powerful proponent of one answer. The upside of this approach is that it makes decisive use of expert contributions. The downside of overemphasizing this approach, without making room for diversity and inclusion, are that it produces groupthink (answers that the whole group supports but that are incorrect) or repudiation (answers that many members of the group do not support).

In horizontal facilitation, by contrast, participants say: "We each have our own answer." Facilitators employ dialogic processes that give space for *inquiring* about these multiple answers and giving space for them to coexist. The upside of this approach is that it includes diverse contributions. The downside of overemphasizing this approach, without making room for expertise and decisiveness, is that it produces cacophony and indecisiveness.

Transformative facilitation cycles between two poles to get the best of both and avoid the worst. The facilitator moves back and forth between advocating for a particular process—forthrightly presenting their perspective on what is happening in the group and what the group needs to do about this—and inquiring as to the perspectives of the participants on these matters. In doing this, they encourage participants to move back and forth between advocating and inquiring about the content of their work: what is happening in the situation and what the group needs to do about this. The participants agree on some answers and disagree on others. Cycling between advocating and inquiring unblocks contribution (by providing space for participants to offer their multiple understandings and to construct a shared one), connection (by providing space for participants to connect and converge their understandings), and equity (by limiting the space for the more powerful to impose their understanding).

To be able to cycle between these two outer moves, the inner shift required of the facilitator—the specific way of paying attention—is *opening*. This means being willing to consider and make sense of multiple perspectives on what is happening and what is needed.

The first basic choice the facilitator must make, then, moment to moment and over and over, is this: Do I focus on advocating or on inquiring?

A GROUP OPENS UP

I got my first good look at what I now call transformative facilitation on a beautiful Saturday afternoon in September 1991 at the homey Mont Fleur Conference Center in the wine country east of Cape Town in South Africa.

(Readers of my previous books will notice that once again I am starting with a story, partly familiar and partly new, from my experience at Mont Fleur. That was my first and seminal experience with transformative facilitation, and I have spent the last thirty years working to make sense and use of what I saw there. In this book, though, I am focusing not on what Mont Fleur showed me about solving tough problems, the interplay of power and love, the methodology of transformative scenario planning, or the possibility of collaborating with the enemy, but on what it showed me about the practice of facilitating breakthrough.)

Trevor Manuel was the head of the Department of Economic Policy of the African National Congress (ANC), the left-wing liberation movement that just the year before had been legalized by the white racist government. Manuel's department had prepared the ANC's position paper on economic policy for the transition to a nonracial democracy, titled "Growth through Redistribution," which called for boosting economic growth by transferring wealth from the wealthier white minority to the poorer Black majority.

Twenty-eight leaders from across all sectors of South African society—Black and white; opposition and establishment; from the left and right; men and women; from politics, business, and civil society—were participating in a weekend workshop at Mont Fleur to talk about how to effect this momentous transition. I was facilitating the workshop and had asked the participants to get together into small groups to inquire about possible scenarios for the country—not what they wanted to have happen, but what could happen.

I was checking in on different groups working in different rooms of the conference center and walked into the basement recreation room just as Manuel, sitting on a sofa, was explaining a scenario he thought the team needed to consider. "This scenario, comrades, is called 'Growth through Repression,'" he said. "It is a story of a right-wing Black government coming to power in South Africa that, like Augusto Pinochet's in Chile, promotes economic freedom while suppressing political freedom." With this mischievous play on words, Manuel was speculating about what would happen if the ANC, to which he had been loyal his whole adult life, was to abandon its socialist ideology.

Then Mosebyane Malatsi, the head of economics of a rival Black party, the radical Pan-Africanist Congress (PAC; one of their slogans was "One Settler [white person], One Bullet"), stood up to propose a scenario that echoed his party's hope that the Chinese People's Liberation Army would come to the rescue of the opposition's armed forces and help them defeat the white government.

I had directed the participants to respond to proposed scenarios not by saying, "I like this scenario" or "I don't like it," but only by asking, "Why does this scenario occur?" or "What happens next?" When Malatsi told his story, the other members of the group asked these questions; he realized that his story was not plausible, so he sat down and never mentioned it again.

The Mont Fleur workshop brought together lifelong opponents during a period of high-stakes political and ideological contestation. In this context, it was remarkable that Manuel and Malatsi, two leading opposition politicians, were openly questioning their own parties' orthodoxies. They were not insisting, "We have the right answer," nor were they simply saying, "We each have our own answer." Instead, in a relaxed and thoughtful way, they were openly offering their thinking, and listening to the thinking of others. They were both advocating and inquiring, and through these moves cocreating a new shared vocabulary and new shared understanding.

———

There were many such incidents during this workshop, which even two years earlier would have been unimaginable. Since 1948, the country had been ruled by a white nationalist government that implemented the system of racial separation called *apartheid* (the Afrikaans word for "apartness"). Black people, who made up

88 percent of the population, were restricted by law to inferior citizenship, housing, land, transportation, jobs, education, and public amenities, and they were not allowed to move around the country freely, vote, or date or marry outside their racial group. Black opposition organizations were outlawed. This system was enforced by banning, imprisonment, torture, and executions. Opponents of apartheid fought it in the South African parliament and courts, through mass mobilization and armed resistance, and with international boycotts and sanctions. In 1986, the government started to repeal the repressive laws, and in 1990, President F.W. de Klerk released Nelson Mandela (then deputy president of the ANC) from twenty-seven years in prison and legalized the ANC, the PAC, and other opposition parties. The government and the opposition began negotiations, first secretly and then openly, to create a new political dispensation.

By the time of this workshop, then, the country was poised for an epochal transition and transformation, but nobody knew how this would unfold. Negotiations started up and broke down. Opposition groups marched, shadowy gangs rampaged, security forces made arrests, and political leaders were assassinated. The decades-long political logjam, with the minority white government unable to control the majority Black population and the Black opposition unable to overthrow the government, was starting to get unstuck and move. The leaders who came to Mont Fleur did so because they wanted to work together to understand and influence what was going on. They and the country were seized with all the fundamental issues: contribution and power, connection and love, equity and justice.

When I arrived at the conference center and entered the main meeting room, ten rectangular tables had been arranged in a hollow square with the chairs on the outside so that the participants would be looking at one another. I removed the tables along one edge of the square so that now the participants would all be looking at a long wall on which I hung flip-chart paper for them to write on. This simple rearrangement produced a fundamental change in the focus of the group's attention: instead of its being on each other and their individual ideas, it was now on the ideas they would create together.

The conference center was surrounded by lovely grounds and next to a mountain nature reserve. During breaks in the workshop, the participants played volleyball and went for walks. These relaxed encounters were extraordinary in the South African context and produced extraordinary interactions. People who had never been able to talk across racial and partisan lines now did so.

Johann Liebenberg, a white Afrikaner, was the chief labor negotiator for the Chamber of Mines. Mining was the country's most important industry, with its operations intertwined with the apartheid system of economic and social control, so in this team, Liebenberg represented the arch-establishment. One afternoon, he went for a walk with Tito Mboweni, Manuel's deputy in the ANC. Liebenberg later reflected on how surprised he was by the openness of their conversation and by Mboweni inquiring rather than only advocating:

> You went for a long walk after the day's work with Tito Mboweni on a mountain path and you just talked. Tito was the last sort of person I would have talked to a year before that: very articulate, very bright. We did not meet blacks like that normally; I don't know where they were all buried. The only other blacks of that caliber that I had met were the trade unionists sitting opposite me in adversarial roles. This was new for me, especially how openminded they were. These were not people who simply said: "Look, this is how it is going to be when we take over one day." They were prepared to say: "Hey, how *would* it be? Let's discuss it."

Howard Gabriels, a former official of the socialist National Union of Mineworkers, had been Liebenberg's adversary in brutal industry negotiations. He described his encounter with Liebenberg at Mont Fleur:

> In 1987, we took 340,000 workers out on strike, 15 workers were killed, and more than 300 workers got terribly injured, and when I say injured, I do not only mean little scratches. He was the enemy, and here I was, sitting with this guy in the room when those bruises are still raw. I think that Mont Fleur allowed him to see the world from my point of view and allowed me to see the world from his.

Gabriels later reflected on the openness of the first round of scenario brainstorming that included Manuel's and Malatsi's stories:

> The first frightening thing was to look into the future without blinkers on. At the time there was a euphoria about the future of the country, yet a lot of those stories were like "Tomorrow morning you will open the newspaper and read that Nelson Mandela was assassinated" and what happens after that. Thinking about the future in that way was extremely frightening. All of a sudden you are no longer in your comfort zone. You are looking into the future and you begin to argue the capitalist case and the free market case and the social democracy case. Suddenly the capitalist starts arguing the communist case. And all those given paradigms begin to fall away.

In another small-group discussion, Liebenberg was recording on a flip chart while Malatsi of the PAC was speaking. Liebenberg was calmly summarizing what Malatsi was saying: "Let me see if I've got this right: 'The illegitimate, racist regime in Pretoria . . .'"

Liebenberg was able to hear and articulate the provocative perspective of his enemy.

I was astounded by these examples of people working together so productively in the midst of such a complex, confusing, and conflictual context. They were more open and relaxed than I was used to from my previous working experiences in corporations and research institutes, where the words I most often heard and said were, "I have the right answer." The South Africans were not insisting that their perspectives were right and had to prevail, nor were they simply accepting all perspectives as equally valid. They were moving back and forth between advocating for their views and inquiring into those of others.

THE FACILITATORS OPEN UP

The collaboration among the participants who were meeting at Mont Fleur was supported by the transformative facilitation of the facilitators. By *facilitators*, I mean all of us who were supporting this collaboration. The project had been organized by three staff members of the opposition-leaning University of the Western Cape: Pieter le Roux, a white professor of social development; Vincent Maphai, a Black professor of political science; and Dorothy Boesak, a Black community activist. They invited me to help them facilitate this project because they wanted to employ the scenario planning methodology to construct a set of logical stories about possible futures.[1] At the time, I was the head of the global social-political-economic scenario team of Shell, which had pioneered the use of scenarios as a tool for strategic planning to deal with the uncertainty it faced in its business environment. Activist consumers in North America and Europe had been boycotting Shell because it had refused to divest from apartheid South Africa, so when my bosses were asked to lend me to this opposition-initiated project, they agreed immediately.

Mont Fleur marked a turning point in my way of working and being. I have always been a know-it-all, and I enjoy thinking I am right. In school I was confident and got good grades. My university studies in physics and economics and then my first jobs in research and corporate planning trained me to look at problems from outside and above, figure out the right answer quickly, and then advocate for it assertively. I was hired into the Shell planning department because of this training and my expertise in the US electricity and gas industry.

But when I got to Shell I started to work in a new way, because at Shell the role of the planner was not to make the plans but to facilitate the company's executives to do so. Our work was organized with precision and neutrality: contracting with our clients (the executives), conducting open-ended preparatory interviews with them, designing structured agendas for the workshops, and then facilitating these workshops all around the world. We were experts in the process, and the executives were experts in the content; we asked the questions, and they gave the answers.

This was the approach to facilitation that I brought to Mont Fleur, but with some crucial differences. I knew that South Africa was going through a historic transition; le Roux had explained to me that most of the participants they had invited had spent their lives fighting for a better South Africa, with many of them having been in exile or in prison or underground. I didn't know much about South Africa or see myself as having a stake in the country. Furthermore, this wasn't a Shell project, so I didn't come with my own expert view about the right questions for the group to focus on.

I therefore arrived at Mont Fleur with what was, for me, an exceptional level of respectfulness, neutrality, curiosity, humility, and attentiveness. I didn't know it at the time, but I had fallen into the perfect orientation for transformative facilitation, and I have spent the decades since understanding what it was that I did then without realizing it. I had snoozed my "I have the right answer" button, and this allowed me to contribute with greater openness. I still provided my expertise, but without my usual arrogance. I asked ignorant questions. Buddhist teacher Shunryu

Suzuki wrote, "In the beginner's mind, there are many possibilities, but in the expert's mind there are few."[2] I came with a beginner's mind, and the participants noticed this. Gabriels told me, "When we first met you, we couldn't believe that anyone could be so naïve. We were certain that you were trying to manipulate us. But when we realized that you actually didn't know anything, we decided to trust you."

Everyone who participated in Mont Fleur—the participants, the other facilitators, and I—showed up with expertise that was important for the work that we were doing. We were all confident that we knew something that others needed to learn. And we also all showed up with openness. Many of the participants had fiercely held positions that they had fought for, taking big risks and expending a lot of energy for a long time. But at Mont Fleur, through some combination of the historic opportunity, the nonpartisan framing of the project, and the peaceful venue in beautiful nature, they relaxed into the unknowns and opportunities in their problematic situation. This relaxation is what surprised Liebenberg about his conversation with Mboweni: "Hey, how *would* it be? Let's discuss it." The three organizers all had well-established political perspectives, but, without concealing these, had conscientiously convened a team that represented the diversity of the South African society (beyond their own friends and allies), and they treated everyone who came with warmth and respect. I brought Shell's well-established methodology and also my humility and curiosity. The openness of each person enabled that of the others, and this enabled us together to create the new connections and new contributions that created new possibilities for the country.

The opening at Mont Fleur created powerful new possibilities because the facilitators systematically reduced the obstacles to collaboration. The purpose of the project was to find ways for South Africans to break through the oppressive stuckness of the apartheid system. We enacted this purpose through creating a united and egalitarian social island: all participants had an equal opportunity to contribute to all sessions, they ate all their meals together, and everyone shared the same type of modest bedroom with another participant. These moves dramatically unblocked contribution, connection, and equity.

The opening up at Mont Fleur also created new possibilities for me. I fell in love with this collaborative way of effecting transformation, with the beauty and vitality of South Africa, and with Dorothy Boesak, the project organizer. The whole experience overwhelmed my habitual sense of apartness. In 1993, I resigned from Shell, emigrated from London to Cape Town, launched into my vocation as a facilitator, and married Dorothy. (Eight years earlier, our interracial union would have been illegal.) Our wedding took place at the Mont Fleur Conference Center—a joyful celebration of new possibilities.

THE KEY TO COMBINING ADVOCATING AND INQUIRING IS OPENING

Opening up enables participants and facilitators to cycle fluidly between advocating and inquiring and thereby to move beyond the vertical pole of "We have the right answer" and the horizontal pole of "We each have our own answer." Opening avoids the vertical downside of a single answer that is incorrect or unsupported and the horizontal downside of a cacophony of answers that are unconnected.

The crucial step that everyone at Mont Fleur took was to pay attention and open up to the possibility that they might not have the right answer. Their opening was supported by the emerging change in the country, which implied that what they did could contribute to creating a new and better future, and by the scenario methodology, which took as its starting point that the future was fundamentally unpredictable and therefore influenceable. Poet Betty Sue Flowers told me that having two scenarios is like having two different pairs of glasses, and that once you become comfortable with two different ways of looking at the world, it is easy to imagine a third or fourth one. The four scenarios the Mont Fleur team constructed enabled them, and the constituencies with whom they shared these narratives, to see more broadly and clearly what was happening, what could happen, and what this meant for what they could and needed to do.

One basic characteristic of all complex and conflictual situations is that they do not simply present problems that have solutions. They are problematic situations that different participants see as problematic from different perspectives and for different reasons, so no stakeholder can have the expertise or credibility to diagnose a problem and prescribe and administer a solution. Advocating for one correct definition of the problem and one correct solution is therefore inadequate.

Collaboration requires engaging with difference and conflict, rather than avoiding them. Participants need to go beyond both the vertical "We have the right answer" and the horizontal "We each have our own answer." Such an approach is required for participants to be able to escape from dead-end answers and discover new ones. The participants in Mont Fleur didn't simply listen to each other empathetically; they also argued fiercely and at length to hammer out their collective contribution to transforming their situation.

THE FACILITATOR MAKES MOVES

The job of facilitators is to provide guidance about process. They can't just make the horizontal statement, "Everyone has their own answer and will do their own thing." Nor can they rely on the vertical dictate, used by fearful beginners, "I have the right answer; you must trust my process." Facilitators can help participants only if they, like participants, move back and forth between bringing their experience and also listening and adjusting to the needs of the situation.

I built up my capacity to make these moves once I had moved to South Africa and started to work as an independent professional facilitator of collaborations within and across companies, civil society organizations, and the new government. I got my first contracts for projects from different members of the Mont Fleur team. One day, for example, I took a short but unusual drive in Johannesburg from a meeting with Liebenberg at the Chamber of Mines to one with Malatsi at the Pan-Africanist Congress. Living and working in South Africa (and being newly married, with four teenage stepchildren) provided many opportunities to learn about working across difference.

As I began to work as a facilitator, I gradually developed the theory and practice of what I now call transformative facilitation in collaboration with a group of researchers associated with the Sloan School of Management at MIT. One foundational model of the MIT body of work is Edgar Schein's process consultation, "which emphasizes the need to involve the client in the process of figuring out what is wrong and what can be done about it."[3] He writes:

> The complex problems of today are not technical ones that can be solved with specific tools. The best we can do is to find workable responses or what I am calling here "adaptive moves." This will involve new kinds of conversations of a more dialogic, open-ended variety. The emphasis on the concept of "moves" is important in this context because it implies action without necessarily having a plan or solution in mind . . . The adaptive move is not another "tool" in the consultant's bag and there are no formulas for "what to do when," because so much depends on the actual situational complexities.[4]

Transformative facilitation focuses on five pairs of moves made by facilitators and participants. The first pair is advocating and inquiring.

———

In 1990, Schein's colleague Peter Senge wrote an influential book called *The Fifth Discipline: The Art and Practice of the Learning Organization*, which synthesized important elements of this body of work, including the importance of balancing inquiry and advocacy.[5] Through Senge, I starting working with a business consultant in South Africa named Louis van der Merwe. The culture of companies there was saturated by verticality: one of our clients told me, showing me his five fingers clenched in a fist, that he had a "five-point plan." Van der Merwe and I worked to apply transformative facilitation in this challenging context, and he gave me the most important lesson first: that although many people thought that facilitation was just a manipulative form of vertical forcing (as Gabriels had said to me), what we were doing was fundamentally different—our role was to enable participants to find their own way forward. At the same time, our approach implicitly embodied an egalitarian and humanistic ideology: that all participants needed to contribute to addressing the problematic situations in which they had a stake.

Van der Merwe taught me a process for a three-day strategy workshop that was based on Senge's writings.[6] I learned how to facilitate these workshops by practicing: I ran fifteen workshops, week after week, for all of the divisional management teams of a large South African industrial company. This process emphasized methodologies for the managers to develop their strategies through advocating and inquiring about the content: check-ins and checkouts that gave everyone an opportunity to contribute their perspectives; a series of conversations using flip charts and sticky notes to make everyone's ideas visible, connect these ideas, and iteratively develop them; and structured steps to prepare proposals and decide which ones to take forward. Within the company's vertical culture, this transformative process enabled participation, learning, and progress.

The workshop process also included methodologies for the facilitators to both advocate for a particular process and to inquire about the participants' opinions about it. We presented the workshop agenda and checked that it met the expectations of the participants. If an issue arose along the way that implied we might need to change the agenda, we transparently negotiated this change with the group. At the end of every day, we asked for written feedback from each person and used this to adjust the agenda for the following day.

We used the same set of open-ended instructions in every workshop, and van der Merwe insisted that we write out our flip charts the evening before we were to use them. I asked him why we didn't just get the flip charts laminated so that we could use them over and over, and he answered that the practice of writing them out was a way for us to rehearse the workshop in our heads, so that we would be ready and relaxed and able to respond as needed to what might arise—to be fully present to the situation. We handwrote everything on flip charts rather than making PowerPoint slides, so that these artifacts could stay visible throughout the workshop, and also to show that these instructions were all drafts and could be reworked as needed. This was my introduction to the small, simple, subtle moves and shifts that are the basis of transformative facilitation.

As a learner facilitator, I was hungry to acquire more methodologies. In his personal library, van der Merwe had a set of the collected workshop exercises published annually by

Pfeiffer & Company, and I pestered him to let me study them. Eventually he carried the whole tall stack over to the kitchen table where I was sitting and told me that I was welcome to read them, but that they wouldn't help me much.

And he was right: over the decades since, I have added new methodologies to my repertoire—perhaps one a year, usually through working with a new colleague who has a different body of experience. But my increasing competence as a facilitator has not mostly come from learning new methodologies. It has come from being attentive, in the specific situations I have been working with, to how best to employ the five pairs of outer moves and the five inner shifts that this book describes.

THE FACILITATOR OPENS UP THEIR TALKING AND LISTENING

When I was at Shell, my facilitation teacher was the head of the scenario department, Kees van der Heijden. In the way he led our team and worked with the company's executives to ensure that our work would be useful to them, he exemplified the approaches I now recognize as process consultation and transformative facilitation.[7] He was both exacting and humble, insisting that we utilize our expertise in scenario and strategy methodologies in a way that would help our clients deal with the issues that were of concern to them.

The key connection between us and the executives was in dialogue interviews, where we asked open-ended questions to elicit their concerns and questions about the problematic situation they were dealing with. Such one-on-one interactions exemplify transformative facilitation: the interviewer-facilitator uses their genuine curiosity to help the interviewee-participant clarify their thinking about what is going on and what they need to do about it.

In this interaction, the crucial skill required of the facilitator is to listen without judgment and with empathy: to hear what the stakeholder is saying, rather than what the facilitator thinks they should be saying. I once sat beside van der Heijden while he was interviewing an executive, and afterwards we compared our notes. I was shocked to see how much of what the executive had said that I had not heard because I had been distracted by my own reactions, judgments, and projections. Listening is simple but not easy.

———

When I later started working as an independent facilitator, one of my collaborators was Otto Scharmer, a colleague of Schein and Senge's at MIT. Scharmer differentiates among four modes of talking and listening: downloading, debating, dialoguing, and presencing.[8]

Downloading

The first mode is downloading. In the downloading mode of talking, people say what they always say, as if they are downloading a recording from the internet. They download because they think that what they're saying is the only thing they can say in this situation, either because they're certain or too polite or frightened to say something new. Downloading is pure advocating and a typical symptom of both vertical facilitation ("The truth is . . .") and horizontal facilitation ("I have my own truth"). Transformative facilitation requires escaping from downloading.

In downloading, people are not listening at all. They are only reloading: waiting for the other person's mouth to stop moving so that they can tell them again what the truth is. They are not hearing what others are saying or what is going on outside themselves; they are paying attention only to their own thoughts about the situation. Maybe they are not even differentiating their thoughts about the situation from the situation itself. They are projecting their thoughts onto the situation: they might imagine they are walking around with a spotlight on their forehead that illuminates what is going on, but actually it is a projector or beamer.

Debating

The second mode of talking and listening is debating. The debating mode of talking is a clash of ideas: each person says what they think ("In my opinion . . ."). The debating mode of listening is from the outside, factually and objectively, like a judge in a debate or a courtroom ("This is correct and that is incorrect"). This mode is more open than downloading because people are now expressing and listening to different views and are aware that these are views and not simply truths. Debating engages both advocating and inquiring.

Dialoguing

The third mode of talking and listening is dialoguing. The dialoguing mode of talking is self-reflective ("In my experience . . ."). This kind of talking involves not only "I think" but also "I feel" and "I want." The dialoguing mode of listening to others is as if from inside them, empathetically and subjectively ("I hear where you are coming from"). Dialoguing engages, more openly, advocating and inquiring.

Presencing

The fourth mode of talking and listening is presencing. This neologism combines pre-sensing (sensing what is in the process of coming into being) and being fully present (attentive and undistracted). Here people listen not simply from the perspective of one or another person, but from the larger system ("What I am noticing here and now is . . ."). When I am in a group that is presencing, it is as if the boundaries between people have disappeared, so that when one person talks, they are articulating something for the whole group or system, and when I listen, it is to the whole group or system. Presencing is a fully open way of engaging advocating and inquiring.

A few years after I had moved to South Africa, Dorothy and I co-facilitated a strategy workshop for the regional Synod of Anglican Bishops. On the first day, we were talking about norms for the meeting that would enable them to move beyond downloading: beyond reproducing their existing perspectives and positions. One bishop suggested, "We must listen to one another." A second said, "No, brother, that's not quite it. We must listen with empathy." Then a third said, "That's still not quite what we need. We must listen to the sacred within each of us." With these three suggestion, the bishops echoed Scharmer's model of debating, dialoguing, and presencing. Presencing is talking from and listening to the highest potential of the group or system.

THE FACILITATOR OPENS UP THROUGH MAKING THREE SHIFTS

I have found Scharmer's model to be particularly useful in its description of three specific practices for shifting from more closed to more open modes of talking and listening: suspending (opening your mind), redirecting (opening your heart), and letting go (opening your will).

Suspending

Suspending is a crucial practice because it's the first move away from the downward spiral of vertical and horizontal downloading and toward transformative facilitation. Suspending means that a person is acknowledging that their thoughts about what is happening may not be accurate descriptions of what is actually happening. They are taking their thoughts and hanging them in front of themselves, as if from a string, so that they and others can see and ask about these thoughts, and so that they can, if they wish, change them. When Manuel told the story of "Growth through Repression," he was suspending his party's platform of "Growth through Redistribution," which he later helped reshape. When Malatsi told his China story to the group and then chose to listen to their questioning, he was suspending his party's official line, which he also later helped reshape.

Suspending is such an important practice for transformative facilitation that many of the exercises Reos uses in workshops are specifically designed to demonstrate and enable it. For example, we often ask participants to write their ideas on sticky notes, sheets of flip-chart paper, or a physical or virtual whiteboard, which can be easily viewed and questioned by everyone, rearranged, rewritten, and perhaps discarded or erased. We also ask them to use toy bricks to construct physical models that represent their individual and collective thinking about their current situation and how they could change it, which enables people to make and revise their ideas (and the connections among them) more easily and fluidly than they would having to negotiate the right words to write down.[9] By enabling participants to suspend their thinking, all these methods enable them to move fluidly between advocating and inquiring and thereby to advance.

Another exercise for suspending is to use collaborative feedback. A group of people who have been working on something present the draft results to a second group. The second group gives feedback and asks questions. The first group must write down this feedback but must not give any answers at all. (Afterward the two groups switch roles, and then they confer separately and decide on what they want to do with the feedback they've gotten.) Both sides of this exercise are unconventional: the second group must give feedback intended to be helpful, not (as is common) to show

how smart they are, and the first group must listen to the feed-back to see what is useful, not (as is common) to take up all of their time re-explaining and defending their results. This exercise emphasizes suspending in order to encourage helpfulness and progress.

Playing also helps us relax our tight hold on our ideas. My colleague Ian Prinsloo, a former theater director, has taught me how valuable purposeful games and icebreakers can be because they reduce hierarchy and formality, which impede contribution, connection, and equity and therefore limit creative collaboration.

It takes care to create a physical-political-psychological space within which participants can feel safe enough to relax and pay attention to what is happening right then and there, rather than being distracted by what happened another time or is happening somewhere else. This is why we suggest the group ground rule or norm of "Be present" and ask participants to turn off and put away their cell phones. Downloading is living within your own bubble of thoughts, preoccupations, and habits; suspending requires stepping out of that bubble and seeing afresh what is happening around you.

Redirecting

The second practice, to move from debating to dialoguing, is redirecting. Redirecting means listening not from outside but from inside another. For example, when I am struggling to listen empathetically in a dialogue interview with a stakeholder, I imagine myself literally speaking from inside them. Gabriels was referring to redirecting when he said that his encounter with Liebenberg "allowed him to see the world from my point of view and allowed me to see the world from his."

Seeing the situation from the perspective of others requires having some kind of connection and relationship with them. This is why we place so much emphasis on activities that enable informal, horizontal, personal connections. At Mont Fleur these included eating and drinking together (a neighboring winery had donated several cases of excellent South African wine) and going for mountain walks. We often also hold sessions where participants can share personal stories from their lives that in some way illuminate the subject we are speaking about, which both help all participants to see their situation from other perspectives and to connect with one another more personally.

In 1986, the American humanistic psychologist Carl Rogers visited South Africa to deliver a series of trainings, which van der Merwe attended and later referred to often. Rogers's skill in empathetic listening was legendary; his therapeutic approach emphasized treating others with "unconditional positive regard."[10] But in one public meeting with facilitators, Rogers was asked a question about race by a young blond, blue-eyed white man. Rogers noticed that he was having trouble hearing the man because of dynamics within himself, and he had to ask the man to repeat his question several times. Eventually Rogers apologized, saying "I can't hear you. It must be something in me that is preventing me from hearing you." Apparently even Rogers had limits to his capacity for redirecting. Later in that lecture, Rogers made a statement that van der Merwe often emphasized as a foundational assumption of transformative facilitation: "I have an unshakeable belief in the wisdom of a group to know what it has to do next—provided that all of the resources of the group are available to it." A group can find its way forward if and only if it unblocks equitable contribution and connection.

Letting Go

The third practice, to move from dialoguing to presencing, is letting go. A team can sometimes make progress by agreeing, through debating or dialoguing, with a perspective or option that one of them had come up with previously. But more often they need to create new perspectives or options together. My experience of this shift to presencing is that we all see something that's important, but it comes not from one of us but from among us, as if it were growing from the middle of our circle. This requires letting go, at least for a while, of our own ideas and stories. This was the confusing experience Gabriels referred to when he said that "all of those given paradigms began to fall away," and that I had when my habitual protective shell was cracked open by my experience at Mont Fleur. The "Icarus" scenario, a story about the populist economic policies crashing the economy, which was the project's most important contribution to the national debate about the transition, was the product of such letting go, especially by Manuel, Mboweni, and Malatsi, who had been fiercely guarding their parties' economic policies that this scenario put into question.

Opening up creates new possibilities

Facilitators employ, model, and teach opening—to enable cycling between advocating and inquiring, to understand what is going on, and so to be able to make well-grounded decisions about what to do next. Furthermore, opening is foundational for all four of the other pairs of moves and for the other four shifts.

My experience of opening at Mont Fleur enabled me to discover the transformative facilitation approach and also my vocation to employ and develop this approach. But the opening I experienced then, and other breakthroughs I have made since, weren't accomplished once and for all. I have had to practice these moves and learn these lessons over and over; often I have found a way forward and then lost it and had to refind it.

After the workshop in Colombia where I had spoken with Francisco de Roux, he invited me to give a seminar on Reos's methods to the just-appointed members of his Truth Commission. Each of them had different passionately held views about what they needed to do to accomplish their daunting mission to enable national healing, and de Roux insisted that I present the model of the four modes of talking and listening. We did a short exercise that involved trying out these modes in sequence. Then I asked the participants whether the exercise had changed anything for them, and one of them gave a simple, practical answer: "I discovered that I had more options than I realized I had." At the end of the seminar, de Roux summarized what the group had accomplished: "It seems to me that our situation has become more malleable, like Play-Doh does as you knead it."

In transformative facilitation, facilitators practice *opening* their talking and listening, and in doing so encourage participants to do the same. This foundational practice of transformative facilitation enables everyone to move fluidly back and forth between *advocating* and *inquiring* and thereby to continue to deepen their understanding of what is happening and what they need to do. Over the course of the unfolding of a collaboration, facilitators and participants need to keep making these moves and this shift, over and over.

7

How Do We Define Success?
Concluding and Advancing

*T*he purpose of transformative facilitation is to help people transform their problematic situation. The second question that the collaborators need to work with, repeatedly, is: How do we define success in transforming our situation?

In vertical facilitation, participants define success as *concluding*: making a deal, pact, or agreement. They say, "We need to agree." The facilitator focuses on enabling such agreement. The upside of this approach is that it provides a clear and definitive finish line to work toward. The downside of overemphasizing this approach, without making room for pragmatism about what agreements are possible and useful, is that it defines a window of success that may be too narrow: reaching an agreement may be more than the collaboration is able to accomplish (because the participants are not willing or able to agree), or it may be less (because the participants want to go beyond making an agreement, to achieve other results).

In horizontal facilitation, the participants define success as *advancing*. They say, "We each just need to keep moving forward, whether together or separately." The facilitator focuses on enabling such movement. The upside of this approach is that it focuses on taking pragmatic next steps, even if they are partial or messy or don't include everyone. The downside of overemphasizing this approach, without a clear finish line, is that it values activity over results, so participants may find that the results they end up producing are unsatisfyingly dispersed and insubstantial.

As I said in the previous chapter, transformative facilitation cycles between two poles to get the best of both and avoid the worst. Here the facilitator helps participants move back and forth between reaching tentative conclusions and building on these conclusions to continue to advance.

To be able to cycle between these two outer moves, the inner shift required of the facilitator—the specific way of paying attention—is *discerning*. This means working thoughtfully with the dimension of time—being attentive to when to slow down and when to speed up, when to agree and when to agree to disagree, when to keep the work unformed and fluid and when to grasp the solidity that has crystallized, and ultimately when to conclude and end the collaboration.

The second basic choice the facilitator must make, then, moment to moment and over and over, is this: Do I focus on concluding or on advancing?

A GROUP CHOOSES NOT TO AGREE

In June 2004, in the town of Bergen in the Netherlands, we held the kickoff workshop for a two-year project called the Sustainable Food Laboratory.[1] The purpose of this project was to make mainstream food systems more sustainable. The workshop included leaders of regional farmer organizations, global food companies, retailers, banks, philanthropic foundations, government agencies, and environmental and development nongovernmental organizations, from across the Americas and Europe. They had all come to the workshop because they were concerned that the mainstream food system was or could soon become unsustainable, from one perspective or another: soil loss, water pollution, diminishing biodiversity, insecure supply chains, unaffordability, consumer dissatisfaction, vulnerable local economies, or farmer or farmworker livelihoods and health. They also had deep and long-standing disagreements about which of these issues mattered most and what needed to be done. For example, they disagreed about whether it was important to support smallholder farming or to promote industrial farming.

The workshop went well. The participants were happy to be meeting one another across their differences and to be looking at their situation from multiple angles. We had organized panel presentations, whole-group dialogues, breakout sessions, and field trips to interesting nearby farms and food factories and shops. The group was enthusiastic about the prospect of working together to discover and implement ways to deal with the problematic situation they all cared about.

On the last day, during a plenary conversation that I was facilitating, one participant said that before we could go further we needed as a group to agree on our definition of *sustainable*. This suggestion sounded logical to me: the group would not be able to agree on how to advance until they agreed on what constituted advancing. But I also sensed that at this early point in their process, the group's shared understanding and trust were inadequate to agree on such a complicated and important matter, and that trying to do so would break the collective momentum they were building.

The participants decided not to try to agree on the definition, and we kept going. In spite of or because of this ambiguity, they carried on working together and have continued to do so for more than fifteen years; they have found the process valuable for much longer than the two years the initiators, Hal Hamilton and I, had originally envisaged. Over this period they have made important contributions to achieving a more sustainable mainstream food system, including in managing water supplies and greenhouse gas emissions, improving the environmental and social performance of commodity supply chains, reducing food waste, and increasing the incomes of smallholder farmers. It turns out that it is possible to make a lot of useful advances even if certain basic matters are not precisely agreed on.

The Food Lab participants and facilitators have succeeded in cycling between concluding and advancing. They are pragmatic people and are committed to producing results on the ground. Their connections to agriculture provided them with helpful metaphors for this cyclical or seasonal rhythm: that patient cultivation is required to enable new things to grow; that growth can be enabled (especially through removing obstacles) but not forced; that learning about how to enable growth often comes from hands-on trial and error; and that things that don't grow (that die) can nonetheless be composted to provide nourishment for the next trial. Hamilton told me that the tension around agreeing on objectives for Food Lab initiatives has persisted throughout. On the one hand, defining measurable goals provides clarity that enables initiatives to be approved by sponsors and to be managed. On the other hand, such definitions often constrain them to producing smaller or narrower results.

I notice this same creative tension in my role as a manager. Reos Partners is a global social enterprise that operates through ongoing collaboration among multiple legally independent entities located around the world. We move forward together through a continuous back and forth between acting separately according to the imperatives that each entity perceives (sometimes not fully in alignment), and making agreements (sometimes complicated compromises) to come into alignment. Sometimes we choose to keep going in spite of disagreement, and sometimes we stop to resolve a disagreement. This not-straightforward cycling between concluding and advancing requires discernment.

A GROUP CHOOSES TO AGREE

Sometimes, as in the Food Lab workshop, a group finds it more important to advance than to agree. Other times the opposite is true, and an agreement is needed. My colleagues and I had been working for four months with a team of civic leaders from South Carolina on how to transform their chronically ineffective and inequitable primary and secondary education system. Now they were meeting just before they were to present their conclusions in a public meeting, and hundreds of years of pain and polarization suddenly came to a head. Their disagreement was about one word in the text they were about to share, one word that exposed the deep-rooted schisms in the team and in the system they represented and were trying to change.

One member of the team, a conservative white businessman, raised an objection to including the word *racism* in the presentation because he thought it unfairly blamed present-day white people for historical injustices. Another member, a Black female school administrator, became upset at his unwillingness to acknowledge the ongoing, systemic white privilege and discrimination against Black people that she had both witnessed and suffered from. Tension in the room surged, but the team thought that now their presentation needed to be unambiguous on this point, and they agreed to include the word. This presentation and project were pivotal in the transformation of this school system.

In order to make progress, groups often need to agree and conclude. Choosing one or a few solutions out of many possible solutions involves culling or cutting. Facilitators need to guide this carefully—perhaps through multiple iterations of deliberations by the whole group or a committee, along with polling or voting—to avoid a choice that is premature or that fractures the group.

GROUPS CAN ADVANCE BY CYCLING BETWEEN AGREEING AND NOT AGREEING

I have observed this tension and cycling between concluding and advancing over several decades in my work with several groups trying to create peace in Colombia. In 1995, long before the 2017 workshop I referred to in the introduction, I was invited by businessman Manuel José Carvajal and politician Juan Manuel

Santos to speak about my experience at Mont Fleur to a group in Bogotá that was interested in organizing a similar project for Colombia. At the time, the national armed conflict was at its peak, and the people in the room included a broad range of leaders from across these divisions: different political parties, the military, businesspeople, academics, and left- and right-wing rebels and warlords. A leader of the FARC guerilla movement also joined the meeting by telephone from hiding in the mountains outside the city. When I finished my presentation, the guerilla asked me a question I wasn't prepared for: Would the FARC have to agree to a ceasefire in order to participate in the proposed workshops? I thought about this and replied that the only requirement for participating was a willingness to listen and talk. My answer satisfied him.

In 1996, the Destiny Colombia project got under way. Four leaders of the illegal guerilla groups were invited to participate, and the government offered them safe passage to the workshops, but the guerilla leaders feared a trap and so participated in nine days of workshops by speaker phone (three from prison, one from an unknown location outside the country)—an early, effective example of undertaking a complex collaboration with a distributed group. Their involvement helped the project and the report it produced, about different options for addressing the conflict, make a contribution to its later resolution.[2] In this case, requiring agreement in advance on a major aspect (a ceasefire) of the intended result of the effort (a resolution of the conflict) would have prevented the group from even getting started on the effort. So, as in the Food Lab, not agreeing at one time enabled agreeing later on.

Twenty years later, in 2016, Juan Manuel Santos was president of Colombia, and he finally succeeded in signing a set of peace accords with the FARC, for which he was awarded that year's Nobel Peace Prize. On the day his award was announced, he referred to that first 1995 meeting as having been "one of the most significant events in the country's search for peace."[3]

I was delighted that Santos was acknowledging our work, but didn't understand why, after all those years, he had done so. So many larger efforts to resolve the conflict had taken place over the intervening decades: dozens of local mediations, an enormous military campaign to pacify the country (which he had directed while minister of defense), and years of negotiations between the government and FARC.

A few months later I was in Bogotá to conduct a public interview of Santos, and I asked him why he had mentioned Destiny Colombia. He answered, "I often refer to this project because it is where I learned that, contrary to all of my upbringing, it *is* possible to work with people you do not agree with and will never agree with." I found this reply illuminating because facilitators often imagine that if participants could just meet and talk, they would discover that they actually agree. But Santos was emphasizing a more common and challenging scenario: participants who meet and do not agree but still need to find a way to work together.

I wanted to make sure that I wasn't misunderstanding Santos's point, so I asked my Colombian colleague Joaquin Moreno for his interpretation. "Many people view Santos as a traitor," he said. "In Colombia we don't have a culture of 'agreeing to disagree.' If you disagree with me, especially in public, I must destroy you." This is true in many national and organizational cultures, where people define consensus as "You agree with me" and collaboration as "We do it my way."

Santos was making a point that many politicians understand but many others don't: important collaborations often require nonagreement as well as agreement. Events in Colombia since the signing of the detailed 297-page peace agreement underline this point in another way: even though the agreement was celebrated by many people inside the country and internationally, it only ended one phase of the conflict (war between the government and the FARC) and started another (other forms of physical and structural violence). At best, the agreement was an interim result on the road to peace. That conflict, like all complex challenges, is not simply a problem that can be solved: it is a problematic situation that can only be worked with and through.

Marriage researcher John Gottman makes a similar point about nonagreement in couples: "Sixty-nine percent . . . of marital conflict are perpetual, which means they will be part of your lives forever, in one form or another . . . [Happy couples] may not love these problems, but they are able to cope with them, to avoid situations that worsen them, and to develop strategies and routines to deal with them."[4] Gottman's point is that happy couples have the capacity to distinguish between what needs to be agreed on and what simply lived with.

Santos's enthusiasm for the Destiny Colombia project gave me an opportunity to work on another long-standing problematic situation. In 2012, he convinced his thirty-one fellow heads of state of the countries in the Americas to commission a hemispheric multi-stakeholder project to look for new options to deal with "the drug problem in the Americas." The project was organized by the Organization of American States (OAS), and I led the facilitation team.[5] At the beginning I was concerned about this framing of the complex situation—with its interwoven security, health, social, economic, political, and international dimensions—simply as a problem. But as I learned more about the history of drug policy, I came to understand that this rigid vertical adherence to one particular definition of the problem (the production, transportation, and consumption of certain intoxicating substances), one particular type of solution (prohibition, interdiction, and criminalization), and one permanent set of agreements (the three international drug control treaties of 1961, 1971, and 1988) were central to the failure of fifty years of efforts to address this situation.

The project was high profile and exciting. We set up a facilitation team of staff from OAS, Reos, and the Colombian Center for

Leadership and Management. Together we convened a team of forty-six leaders from across all the countries of the Americas and the sectors involved in drug policy: politics, security, business, health, education, Indigenous people, international organizations, the justice system, and civil society. The process included two three-day workshops in Panama, but I worked on this project every day for a full year, organizing preparatory and follow-up work, negotiating among the participating governments and participants, drafting documents, and keeping our teams aligned. Facilitating a process to address a problematic situation involves much more than just running workshops.

As our facilitation team began to work together, the differences in our approaches to facilitation came into focus. The culture of facilitation of OAS, an intergovernmental organization staffed by politicians and diplomats, tended to be formal and vertical, and Reos's tended to be informal and horizontal. In the daily back and forth in our team—often tense, sometimes fun—we enacted productive transformative facilitation.

The workshops, with a big group coming together to deal with a complex and important subject using an unfamiliar approach over three long days, were complicated and heated. After one session when I had been fully attentive and in flow, successfully discerning when to conclude and when to advance, one of my colleagues observed approvingly that I had "dominated the field" like a great soccer player. This image of moving back and forth, quickly and fluidly, working with the situation as it arises, is a good illustration of the practice of transformative facilitation.

One important and unusual thing happened during the second workshop. The participants were converging on a set of innovative conclusions about three different ways, rather than one single way, of defining "the problem" (as security coordination, public health, or community cohesion), each of which implied a different kind of solution. Then one participant proposed a fourth, radical option that defined the problem as unfair international treaties that were causing drug-transiting countries such as

Mexico to suffer as a result of the demand from drug-consuming countries such as the US, which implied a solution of abrogating the treaties.

Usually, once a group is close to concluding ("We need to agree"), they are reluctant to incorporate a new idea. I thought this new idea might be valuable and suggested that the participant who proposed it develop it further with a few others. He did so and brought it back to the whole group to advocate for it three times before they agreed to include it in their final report, over the fierce opposition of the governments (especially the US government) that did not want the treaties to be questioned.

The report of this project opened up a previously closed debate about drug policy among governments in the hemisphere and globally, with different governments experimenting with different policies to address their own situation ("We each need to move forward").[6] In this project, then, both within this workshop and in the larger intergovernmental process, the participants were only able to discuss new options once they were able to reconsider previous agreements.

———

If reaching agreements is one pole of facilitating, what is the other? It is finding ways to move forward while staying in relationship. In the first workshop of the Food Lab, we discerned that at that early stage in our collaboration, it was more important to form the group and begin to work together than it was to try to reach a conclusion. In the second workshop of the drug policy project, the productive working relationships that the participants had formed enabled them to reopen their conclusions to incorporate a late, divergent addition. As these two examples illustrate, social innovation usually does not result simply from coming up with new ideas but from forming new relationships, connections, and alliances that enable new or old ideas to be implemented.

I saw this principle in action in Mexico on September 19, 2017, when a magnitude 7.1 earthquake struck Mexico City and the surrounding areas, killing almost four hundred people and injuring six thousand. At that time, I was working with two different teams of Mexican participants on issues related to insecurity, illegality, and inequity. (I describe this project further in the next chapter.) My colleagues and I had been working with one team for two years and the other for only two months. Each team had its own WhatsApp channel, and when the earthquake hit, they both immediately began chatting about what had happened and what should be done. In reading through both channels in real time on that day and the days that followed, I was struck by the difference in their emphases. The emphasis of the newer team was blaming: for example, which politicians and government departments were responding ineffectively and who had corruptly issued substandard building permits. The emphasis of the older team was on collaborating—for example, someone was arranging for supplies to be delivered to Puebla and wanted to know whom her driver should contact upon arrival. The older team members were not in agreement with one another—even after years, their ideological differences were just as sharp as they had been when they first started working together—but they had come to know and trust one another and were therefore able to get important things done together. Relationships enable progress.

DISCERNING ENABLES CYCLING BETWEEN CONCLUDING AND ADVANCING

There is a simple model that is useful for describing and facilitating collaborative creative processes. It posits that a group of participants can create something new—new understandings, relationships, commitments, or initiatives—by working through three stages. The first stage is diverging: each person contributing their experiences, ideas, or perspectives. The second is emerging:

letting these different perspectives connect and cook until a shared set of perspectives or maybe a common perspective becomes clear. The third is converging: drawing conclusions and making agreements.

This model is useful at two scales. For a single creative activity, such as a session in a workshop, it emphasizes that we create something new during the second stage, and that we must not short-circuit this by moving directly from the first to the third: by moving directly from presenting a range of options to choosing from among these (as many methodologies do). This second phase is always unclear and often uncomfortable, so one important challenge for facilitators and participants is to have the patience to stay in this ambiguity long enough for something new to emerge. Contrary to the conventional vertical approach, it is often neither necessary nor productive for participants to agree at each step before they proceed to the next. Frequently they discover that a matter they were disagreeing about no longer seems important—so a crucial area for discernment is between what they do and don't need to agree on.

The poet John Keats had a term for this crucial capacity to stay patiently in nonconclusion until you discern that it is time to conclude: *negative capability*, which he defined as "being capable of being in uncertainties, mysteries, and doubts without any irritable reaching after fact and reason."[7] This capability is crucial to being able to cycle between concluding and advancing. In the first Food Lab workshop, for example, trying to converge immediately on a common definition of sustainability would have cemented the differences among the participants; instead, they stayed in not-knowing long enough to be able to act and learn together—as they did, fruitfully, over the months and years that followed.

The three-phase model is also useful in facilitating a process over time, where these phases are repeated at different scales, such as over a single activity, over a sequence of activities within a meeting, and over an arc of the work across multiple meetings. So a process of collaboration will often be punctuated by many convergences and agreements that mark the end of one activity and the beginning of another. In the drug policy project, for example, the stakeholder team diverged, emerged, and finally converged on their final report, and this report opened up a new cycle of diverging and emerging in the larger hemispheric community of drug policymakers.

In transformative facilitation, the facilitator and the participants employ repeated cycles of diverging, emerging, and converging, and of *concluding* and *advancing*, to move forward together. This requires *discerning*.

8

How Do We Get from Here to There? Mapping and Discovering

*T*ransformative facilitation supports a group in undertaking a journey to transform their problematic situation. The third basic question they need to work with is: How will we get from where we are (the subject of the first question) to where we want to be (the subject of the second)?

In vertical facilitation, the participants say about the steps they will take to make progress on their problematic situation, "We know the way." The facilitator says the same about the process the participants will employ as they take these steps. The upside of this approach of *mapping* a route is that it provides a clear way forward. The downside of overemphasizing this approach, without being open to changing the route along the way, is that it can lead the group into a dead end or off a cliff: the chosen route may not work, but the group will persist in following it nonetheless.

In horizontal facilitation, the participants and the facilitator, knowing how challenging it is to predict and commit to a future series of collective actions, say: "We will find our way as we go." The upside of this approach of *discovering* the route along the way is that it recognizes that collaborative processes are often uncontrollable and unpredictable, and therefore need to be developed democratically and step-by-step. The downside of overemphasizing this approach, without planning out the route in advance, is that it produces disorganized and divergent wandering.

Here again, transformative facilitation cycles between two poles to get the best of both and avoid the worst. The facilitator works with participants to move back and forth between mapping out the route they plan to follow and discovering along the way how they need to modify this plan. To cycle between these two outer moves, the inner shift required of the facilitator—the specific way of paying attention—is *adapting*. This means planning a route, making a move, getting feedback, and adjusting the route accordingly.

The third basic choice the facilitator must make, then, moment to moment and over and over, is this: Do I focus on mapping or on discovering?

Progress involves failing

In November 2015, during the first workshop of the Possible Mexicos project, our facilitation team had a fierce argument. In 2014, Mexico had been rocked by a series of corruption scandals and massacres, and hundreds of thousands of people had taken to the streets in protest. A group of committed citizens got together to organize an ambitious multi-stakeholder process to find ways to deal with this nexus of "the three I's": illegality, insecurity, and inequity. They engaged Reos to help facilitate this process.

This first workshop brought together a group of thirty-three national leaders: politicians, human rights activists, army generals, business owners, religious leaders, trade unionists, intellectuals, and journalists. The facilitation team consisted of twelve Mexican organizers and five Reos staff members. The Reos team had mapped out a complicated agenda for the workshop, which involved both an innovative sequence of plenary and breakout conversations and also a set of parallel learning journeys by subgroups of participants to visit nearby communities to hear about their experiences of the three I's.

Everyone in the workshop felt the pressure of this complex and contentious collaboration. During the second day, some of the participants felt confused and frustrated by the unfamiliar process, and some of the organizers became worried that the workshop and the project might fail. The facilitation team discussed this, and then over dinner, a committee of five of us (three from Mexico, two from Reos) sat together and reworked the details of the agenda for the next day to address the complaints we had heard.

I was pleased that our committee had managed to grasp what was going on and to pivot sharply. But when I presented our new agenda to the larger facilitation team, one of the organizers was indignant. "You don't know what you're doing!" she said. "You are just improvising!"

This produced an argument in the facilitation team that went on in person for an hour on the third day before the workshop restarted, and then by email for another week. I felt torn between, on the one hand, satisfying the expectation of the organizers that Reos, the expert consultants, ought to be able to design and facilitate a process that would work ("We know the way") and, on the other, recognizing that however well we planned, unexpected dynamics would arise and we would have to adjust our plan ("We will find our way as we go"). This tension mirrored a larger one in the country, between a simple hope that some brilliant leaders could direct a good way forward, and the messy uncertainties, complications, and conflicts involved in actually moving forward together.

Boxer Mike Tyson said, "Everybody has a plan until they get punched in the mouth . . . If you're good and your plan is working, somewhere during the duration of that, the outcome of that event you're involved in, you're going to get the wrath, the bad end of the stick. Let's see how you deal with it. Normally people don't deal with it that well."[1] In Mexico, I struggled to deal well with my plan not having worked.

Eventually the argument in our facilitation team subsided, and we agreed to carry on with the project. We continued to work together for more than five years, in different configurations, through many breakdowns and breakthroughs, on different aspects of the three I's, including legal reform, local peacemaking, household worker rights, earthquake preparedness, and public education. We kept having to manage this basic tension between mapping and discovering. We often returned to the well-known phrase of the Spanish poet Antonio Machado: "Walker, there is no path. The path is made by walking."[2]

One of our follow-on projects was the Education Laboratory. Mexico needs to improve its education system to meet the needs of its diverse population and developing economy: high school graduation rates and test scores are low; conflict among education authorities, teachers unions, and civil society organizations is high; and successive governments have attempted ambitious reforms, only to have these reforms reversed when a new administration comes to power. This project brought together fifty leaders from across the national education system—federal and state ministers of education and other government officials, politicians from different parties, teachers union and parents association leaders, principals, teachers, entrepreneurs, academics, and activists—in a multiyear process to identify and implement a set of systemic reforms.

The core of this process was work by nine initiative teams, each composed of five to ten participants and working on a different leverage point in the system at which a small effort could make a big impact. One team, trying to scale up early childhood development programs, included a seasoned researcher and campaigner, one politician with experience in public health programs and another who shepherded an enabling law through Congress, and a technology expert with connections to a state government where the team piloted its strategy. A second team, working on introducing new technology-enabled learning methodologies to reach marginalized communities, included an Indigenous leader with the childhood experience of such marginalization, an education entrepreneur whose understanding of what was needed was shaken up by hearing this leader's story, a hard-driving education ministry project manager, a school principal, and a philanthropist. A third team, working on changing the way resources are allocated to schools, included two senior officials from the education ministry, a congresswoman, and an educational policy expert, who together were able to identify precisely where and when to change the budget allocation rules.

These and the six other teams were powerful because they included diverse and remarkable people who had never before been willing and able to join forces. They reminded me of a team of superheroes, like the Avengers, made up of people with complementary, powerful capacities—including some who up until now hadn't been talking—who can achieve their ambitious objectives only if they collaborate.[3]

Such collaboration requires participants to make difficult choices. Is this a battle that I am willing to join, and in so doing, depart from my familiar way of working? Am I willing to team up with these different others, including those I don't agree with, like, or trust? In order to achieve our mission, am I willing to compromise on something that really matters to me, or even to be seen as a traitor? Collaborating does not involve a single choice—whether to join a team—but a series of them.

Everyone in the Education Lab faced these questions and had to decide, over and over, whether to keep showing up for the project and collaborating. They always had as possible fallbacks the three other, unilateral options for dealing with their situation: forcing, adapting, or exiting. Each member of each project team had a different type of contribution to make and different availability, working style, access to resources, and freedom to maneuver. The project team leaders, who had no formal authority over their members, struggled to keep their teams together and moving forward. The four teams that were most successful in accomplishing their objectives were able to harness and steer the diverse voluntary energies of their team members to achieve the big goals that none of them would have been able to achieve alone.

The tension between mapping and discovering showed up in every initiative team. They started off with an enthusiastic vision for the reform they wanted to accomplish and a plan for how they were going to accomplish it ("We know the way"). But as they tried to move forward, they encountered unexpected difficulties, outside or inside their team, and therefore needed to pause, take stock, adjust their plan, and try again. The job of our facilitation team was to support these initiative teams as they made their way forward.

Our facilitation team also faced this same challenge at the level of the project as a whole. Over and over we had a plan for what to do; some aspects of the plan wouldn't work, and we would have to change it. These changes were often wrenching because they required alterations to people's responsibilities and budgets. The members of our team also had to decide, over and over, whether to keep showing up for the project.

All collaborations face this challenge because no single stakeholder can control the outcome, and no one can know in advance what will work. Things almost always unfold differently than planned. The process of planning—thinking things through in advance—is useful, but participants and facilitators must be willing to change their plans, often. US president and former army general Dwight Eisenhower said, "Plans are worthless, but planning is everything."[4] Adapting is always required.

THE KEY TO CYCLING BETWEEN MAPPING AND DISCOVERING IS ADAPTING

At their second workshop, the Education Laboratory participants got a taste of the discipline of experimenting and adapting that they needed to be able to advance through trial and error, by playing an improvisation game called "Learning Like a Dolphin." We invited one of them to volunteer to be "the dolphin," which Carlos Cruz (an accomplished community organizer) did, and he was asked to leave the room. The others—the trainers—agreed on a simple series of coherent actions they wanted the dolphin to learn to do: picking up a chair, then moving it to under a window, then sitting on it. The dolphin came back into the room and tried to discover what he was supposed to do. No one was allowed to talk or signal, but the trainers could clap when the dolphin was getting closer to performing the correct action.

This game highlights a crucial competence for transformative facilitation: the ability to experiment and pivot. In the game, the behavior of the trainers is important, because the dolphin can't learn if the trainers give confusing or contradictory feedback. I've seen trainers who are disciplined and conscientious in their clapping and thereby help the dolphin succeed, and others who are inattentive and flippant and leave the dolphin confused and floundering.

The behavior of the dolphin is also crucial. The dolphin role is stressful: Cruz became nervous, sweating heavily, as he struggled to figure out how to succeed. The key is for the dolphin to keep experimenting with different actions and then adapt by building on the ones that elicit strong, affirming claps. The dolphins who fail are those who become stuck: paralyzed, just standing still and thinking, or doing the same incorrect action over and over, even though they're not getting claps. Cruz struggled and succeeded.

In all domains of activity—relationships, business, politics, art—people often get mired in old ways of doing things and fail to find new ways forward. They get unstuck only when they try something different and keep doing so until they discover what works. This is what a soccer player does as she kicks a ball down a crowded field, what a scientist does as she articulates and tests a series of hypotheses, and what an entrepreneur does as she makes different offers to the marketplace. This is what the documentary *The Mystery of Picasso* reveals Pablo Picasso did as he applied paint to a canvas, stepped back, looked at it, and repeatedly painted over what he had done before, searching for the right expression of what he was trying to create.[5]

The discipline required to discover a way forward is, therefore, to try something out, step back and look at the result, and then change it, iterating over and over. I learned this discipline through writing books, where even if I have spent months thinking about and outlining what I want to say, it is only when I write it out, print it out, and look at and get feedback on what I have written that I can know what makes sense and what I need to rewrite and to write next. I can produce a good text only by reworking a bad text a hundred times.

When participants and facilitators engage in a creative collaboration, they need to be able to pivot fluidly, not only individually but as a group, like starlings flying in murmurations. I was pleased with the adjustment the small process committee had made in the middle of the first Possible Mexicos workshop, because when we saw that what we were doing was not working well enough, we quickly and fluidly discerned together what we could do differently, we did it, and it worked better. In transformative facilitation, such responsive improvisation is therefore a sign not of failure but of success.

EXPERIMENTING REQUIRES PIVOTING

Facilitators and participants cannot and need not always do things right the first time, but they do need to learn from what happens and find ways to do better the next time. At the end of every unit of the work of my facilitation teams—every workshop day, project phase, or quarter—we pause for a "plus-delta" meeting (delta is the mathematical symbol for change) in which everyone answers two questions about themselves, their colleagues, and the whole team: "What did I/you/we do well that

I/you/we need to keep doing?" and "What do I/you/we need to do better next time?"

The delta question should not be focused on what the facilitation team did wrong, because they'll rarely have an opportunity for a do-over; it should look ahead at how they need to adapt and what they need to do differently. Most of the time, self-assessments and assessments by others will be congruent and not require much discussion. Sometimes, though, perceptions will differ, and the group will have to work through this to decide what to do next. They must try not to make the same mistakes twice.

When working on complex challenges, facilitators need to try doing new things and doing old things in new ways. They need to try small experiments in safe contexts before trying big experiments in dangerous contexts. A facilitator can improvise well only if they have practiced a lot.

During the meeting of our facilitation team during the first Possible Mexicos workshop, I thought things were going well, but some of my colleagues knew they weren't, so they insisted we sit down, listen carefully to the participants and one another, and work out what to do next. Often, a facilitator can't rely only on their own perspective—they have to ask for feedback from colleagues, clients, and anyone else involved with the situation they're trying to work with. They can ask casually and formally, verbally and in writing, and with specific and open-ended questions. They then need to share all of this feedback with everyone on the team so that they can make grounded individual and collective decisions about what to do next.

Carlos Cruz was clear that the Possible Mexicos team needed robust conversations to be able to pivot: "In this group," he said, "we mustn't be afraid to fight and argue. I don't come here to find friends—I have those in my neighborhood—but rather to find allies. Let's be prepared to challenge each other and to be challenged, so that we can become smarter and stronger and more effective in the vital and difficult work that we are doing." He put his finger on a typical weakness in efforts to collaborate with diverse others: thinking that in order to make progress in such contexts, we need to ignore, avoid, or smother conflicts—to be polite and to paper over our differences (even if this means maintaining a problematic status quo). We are afraid that if we open up this Pandora's box, we will get hurt, and collaboration will be impossible. But papering over the differences in our perspectives, interests, and needs does not make them disappear. It means they will fester and erupt later with greater violence.

The limitation of feedback is that most people don't learn from it. They are frightened of threats to their position or image (or self-image), of failing or of being a failure, so they work to deny negative assessments. I usually find critical feedback painful and so shy away from it. In the Possible Mexicos meeting, though, I was attentive and relaxed enough to be able to recognize my habitual response and to change what I was doing.

In the Education Lab, the system reform projects that the team members were trying to implement were ambitious, but their biggest challenges lay within themselves. At the end of a year of working together, one education ministry official said: "I entered this lab believing that I was flexible and open and able to get to agreements. But I have found that I wasn't as good as I thought I was, and that for us to make progress I needed to change." Every one of us had to pay attention, listen to feedback, work with others, act, adapt, and act again, over and over.

PIVOTING REQUIRES FLUIDITY

Trevor Manuel, the South African politician who told the "Growth through Repression" story at the Mont Fleur workshop in 1991, became one of the country's most important political and economic leaders. After Nelson Mandela was elected president in 1994, Manuel served for twenty years in the national cabinet, first as minister of trade and industry and then as minister of finance and head of the National Planning Commission. In 1999, reflecting on his experiences at Mont Fleur and on the larger transition from apartheid to democracy, he said, "There was a high degree of flux at that time: There was no paradigm, there was no precedent, there was nothing. We had to carve it."[6]

Manuel's choice of words reveals a crucial but underrecognized aspect of trying to effect systemic change. The ancient Greek philosopher Heraclitus said *panta rhei*: "everything is in flux." To carve a situation means to bring forth something new by patiently and gradually working, maintaining a sensitive hands-on connection, with the particular emerging reality in front of you. This is the opposite of forcing the situation into a preformed mold—of downloading an already formed idea of what you think should be emerging. It means moving back and forth between mapping and discovering.

To work together in a way that carves rather than imposes a way forward, what we most need to do is to open up and relax into the work. When we are rigid—when fear of what is happening or could happen causes us to tense up and hold on tight, trying to keep things under control, rather than moving fluidly between mapping and discovering—we prevent ourselves from carving.

Martial arts teacher John Milton once told me that in making a fist in tai chi, I must not clench my hand tightly; it must be loose enough so that I can slip a pencil through it. We clench tightly and hold on to doing things that aren't working because we fear that if we admit, to others or even to ourselves, that what we're doing is wrong, we will get hurt. The key to advancing in the midst of such fear is summoning up the courage to relax enough to be able to adapt.

We can only relax if we are working in a context that enables us to loosen our grip on our habitual patterns of thinking, relating, and acting. In 2003, I facilitated a strategy workshop for the leadership team of the FBI at a government training center outside Washington, DC. The participants were tense. When I asked them at the outset what they were feeling that morning, one replied, "I feel this morning the same way I feel every morning:

frightened that there will be another terrorist attack on New York City." But after a while they took off their jackets and ties and started to relax and have fun building models of their vision for the bureau out of colored paper and pipe cleaners. Then the FBI director, Robert Mueller, came into the room, not smiling—he was late because he had been at the president's daily briefing on intelligence—and immediately all of the team's defensiveness and caution returned. The team's context made it hard for them to relax, so they weren't able to make much progress in this workshop. Transformative facilitation requires fluid cycling, and in some contexts this is particularly difficult to do.

———

When teams are attempting to carve new realities, facilitators must encourage them to experiment openly and playfully in order to learn what happens and what works. The emphasis needs to be less on getting things right the first time and more on being attentive to hearing feedback, adjusting, and trying again. One crucial requirement for such creative experimentation is for the facilitators to organize the physical, political, and psychological space to enable working in this way. This means paying attention to the details of the context and support for the work:

- Organizing the project's sponsorship, framing, and ground rules so that participants feel able to try out new behaviors (I failed to do this for the FBI meeting)

- Setting up the workshop room or its online equivalent with chairs and tables that are small and light, rather than heavy or fixed, so they can easily be moved around into configurations that facilitate new conversations with new people

- Using working materials such as shared flip charts, sticky notes, and toy bricks (and their virtual equivalents), rather than individual notepads or laptops, so that all participants can easily see and use the materials together to regroup and revise their ideas

Methods such as these encourage flexibility within boundaries and enable participants to generate new ideas, relationships, and actions.

This way of collaborating is radically different from the conventional vertical way. The conventional approach is linear and rationalistic: first agree on what the problem is, then the solution, and then a plan to implement the solution (including who will do what); finally, implement the plan as agreed. But in complex and contested situations, the vertical approach does not and cannot work, both because the participants are unlikely to agree on the problem and the solution, and, more fundamentally, because nobody can know what will work until they act.

The practice of transformative facilitation involves gradually and iteratively building consensus and clarity about what is going on in the group's situation (through cycling between advocating and inquiring), where the group wants to get to (through cycling between concluding and advancing), and how they will get there (through cycling between mapping and discovering).

In 1993, after I started working as a professional facilitator, one of my first teachers was David Chrislip. He showed me many of the basics that I still rely on: how to design individual workshops and extended processes, prepare agendas and write legibly on flip charts, and use storytelling and walks.[7] In 2018, I gave a speech where I argued that transformative facilitation is different from conventional vertical facilitation. Chrislip was in the audience, and I was concerned that he would think I was caricaturing the approach he had taught me twenty-five years before. But afterward he told me he agreed: the linear approach to facilitation, where the process is mapped out and agreed to at the beginning, and then followed, is unsuitable for the complex situations participants face increasingly often these days.

This contrast between how we are used to thinking we ought to move forward and how we actually need to move parallels the contrast McGill University management professor Henry Mintzberg observes between the deliberate way business schools teach businesspeople to develop strategies and the emergent way that they actually do. Mintzberg also evokes an image of carving or crafting. "Craft evokes traditional skill, dedication, perfection through the mastery of detail. What springs to mind is not so much thinking and reason as a feeling of intimacy and harmony with the materials at hand, developed through long experience and commitment. Formulation and implementation merge into a fluid process of learning, through which creative strategies evolve."[8] This is the same image Francisco de Roux used at the end of the Truth Commission seminar in Colombia, when he said, "It seems to me that our situation has become more malleable, like Play-Doh does as you knead it."

In transformative facilitation, the facilitator and the participants cycle between *mapping* and *discovering* through active, repeated, iterative, hands-on and hands-dirty experimenting. This requires *adapting* what they are doing as they go.

———

The story of the Education Laboratory has a cautionary coda. After we had been operating for a year, the larger political and economic context of the project shifted, and we started to lose the support of our sponsors, which put all our plans and projects at risk. I had been more focused on the horizontal dynamics within the group than on the vertical demands on the group as a whole, so I was surprised, upset, and angry. In this stressful situation, I became frightened and rigid, and doubled down on the vertical "I know the way." I failed to do exactly what I had been coaching the lab participants to do: learn like a dolphin, listen to feedback, engage with conflict, carve the situation, relax, improvise, experiment, pivot, iterate, learn, and adapt—all easier to advise others to do than to do oneself. Eventually our facilitating team, in consultation with the sponsors, decided that it was time to conclude and close the lab, which we did, with a legacy of some accomplishments and some disappointment. Moving forward together is never straightforward.

9

How Do We Decide Who Does What? Directing and Accompanying

*T*ransformative facilitation helps people collaborate without forcing or being forced, so their actions are both voluntary and coordinated. The fourth question that they need to work with is: How do we decide who does what?

In vertical facilitation, the participants say, "Our leaders decide," and these leaders assign and coordinate the actions of the collaborators. The facilitator supports the leaders in doing this. The upside of this approach is that it provides authorization for and alignment of the actions. The downside of overemphasizing this approach, without making room for self-motivated actions, is that it produces debilitating subordination and resistant insubordination.

In horizontal facilitation, the participants say, "No one is the boss of us: each of us will decide for ourselves what we will do." The facilitator supports the participants in coordinating their independent actions. The upside of this approach is that it respects and harnesses the participants' self-motivated actions. The downside of overemphasizing this approach, without authority and alignment, is that it produces separateness and misalignment.

Here again, transformative facilitation cycles between two poles to get the best of both and avoid the worst. The facilitator helps participants choose and coordinate their actions through employing two modes: *directing* participants, like the director of an orchestra or band, and *accompanying* them, like an accompanist playing piano or drums. To cycle fluidly between these two outer moves, the inner shift required of the facilitator—the specific way of paying attention—is *serving*. When a facilitator is seen to be serving, participants understand and trust that the facilitator's directing, even if strict, is supportive, and that the facilitator's accompanying, even if relaxed, helps them advance. In this way, transformative facilitation enables actions that are both voluntary and coordinated.

The fourth basic choice the facilitator must make, then, moment to moment and over and over, is this: Do I focus on directing or on accompanying?

DIRECTING AND ACCOMPANYING
ARE TWO WAYS TO GET THINGS DONE

In 2010, I began supporting a collaboration in Thailand aimed at addressing the country's critical economic and social challenges, which were entangled in its long-running violent political conflicts. In 2014, our work came to a temporary halt when the military staged a coup d'état. Some of my Thai colleagues thought the junta would be able to contain the conflicts and thereby allow the country to make progress on its challenges, but by 2018 most of them had concluded that the junta had failed to move things forward. One told me that Prime Minister Prayut Chan-o-cha, the former general who had headed the junta and was later elected to lead the government, had complained that he was unable to make the changes he wanted to make. "I have given fifty thousand orders," Prayut said, "but only five hundred have been implemented!"

This comment struck me as significant because I've often spoken with change agents who are frustrated with how hard it is to get things done in their organization or community, and who say, more than half seriously: "If only I were in charge for a day!" But Prayut had been in charge for years and nonetheless struggled to get things done.

Many people, like these change agents, assume that someone is or should be in control and able to provide everyone else simplicity, stability, and security. When things don't go as these people think they should, they lament, "Why don't they"—the government, the bosses, the leaders—"just . . ."

The model of command-and-control, directive, vertical leadership is familiar and straightforward, so it's a popular default. People may wish that it could work, but in many situations it can't, for two interrelated reasons. First, people face situations characterized by irreducible volatility, uncertainty, complexity, and ambiguity—and thus out of their control. Second, in many societies and organizations, people are less bound by hierarchies and less deferential, so they're harder to control. Authoritarian structures such as the Thai junta don't recognize that this shift has occurred and are therefore unable to make much progress on their challenges. Directing by itself has limitations.

In 2018, I heard a story in a Possible Mexicos workshop that illustrated a contrasting, horizontal way that things can get done. Our facilitation team had organized an evening of personal storytelling to help the participants get to know one another better. Many of them had dealt with tough challenges in their lives, and the session was riveting. One story was particularly powerful: a transgender government official narrated how, a decade earlier, she had applied for a job at a big food company and had been ridiculed in the interview and hadn't gotten the job. She spoke sadly and fiercely, and many of us listening to her were moved by this injustice.

Several months later, another team member, an investment banker, was addressing the board of directors of the same company that had rejected the transgender woman. He retold her story and chastised them for their prejudice. The board, already concerned about weaknesses in their employee recruitment, decided to change the company's hiring policy to promote greater equity.

I heard about this incident and asked the banker why he'd chosen to bring this matter up at the company's board meeting. "Once I heard our teammate's story," he replied, "I couldn't not say something. And the story piqued the conscience of the company chairman, and he couldn't not do something." (In this story, the banker acted horizontally in that he decided to take action in his professional sphere of influence, not as a result of any agreement in the Possible Mexicos team. The board then decided to act vertically to implement their new policy.)

The investment banker's actions made a contribution to achieving one of the objectives of the Possible Mexicos project: to increase equity in Mexico. Other team members also chose to take actions, sometimes separately and sometimes together, to achieve the project's objectives. But overall the contribution of these self-initiated and uncoordinated actions was modest. Like vertical directing, horizontal accompanying by itself has limitations. A fundamental challenge of transformative facilitation is how to work with both directing and accompanying such that the participants can succeed in achieving their transformational objectives.

I felt the need to work with both directing and accompanying when I facilitated a complicated three-day workshop about the future of Haiti in January 2021. The event had almost been cancelled the day before because violent protests made it dangerous to travel by road to the venue. The workshop was also technically complicated because of pandemic restrictions on the gathering and because all of the sessions were conducted in Haitian Creole:

thirty-five participants and four local facilitators were together in person at the venue; another ten participated via Zoom from their homes in Haiti, the US, and France, supported by a Haitian facilitator based in Denmark; and I and my Reos colleague Manuela Restrepo facilitated, through an interpreter, from Canada and Colombia, respectively.

This setup placed severe restrictions on Reos's capacity to direct the process, and on many matters we had no choice but to rely on the judgment of our Haitian cofacilitators who could communicate with the participants in Creole and in person. The Reos team had to pay close attention to what was going on in the group, as we could understand it via Zoom and WhatsApp chats, to be able to move back and forth, moment to moment, between directing and accompanying the participants and our cofacilitators.

I also feel the tension between directing and accompanying in my role as a manager in Reos, where I have a limited capacity to make anyone in the company do anything. And in my role as a facilitator of client groups, I have no capacity to make participants do anything; I can direct and accompany them only to the extent they allow me. In both roles, therefore, I need others to connect to the understanding and will that inspires them to act of their own volition.

THE KEY TO COMBINING DIRECTING AND ACCOMPANYING IS SERVING

The transformative facilitator cycles between advising participants what actions (especially process actions) they should take, and supporting them as they take the actions they choose. The facilitator can succeed in doing this only to the extent that they are seen to truly be serving the work of the participants.

In 1993, when I first started working as an independent consultant and facilitator, without the authority I had had as part of
Shell's global planning department, I was mentored by my business partner Bill O'Brien, the retired president of Hanover
Insurance and a pioneer in values-based corporate leadership.
O'Brien was scathing about executives who expect to be served
rather than to serve. He warned me that even the simplest person has a well-tuned "bullshit detector" and cannot be fooled by
inauthentic serving. Participants often think that facilitators are
trying to manipulate them (the cynical term is "facipulation"),
as Howard Gabriels had originally suspected me of doing at
Mont Fleur. Facilitators can serve effectively only if participants
are confident that they are genuinely being served.

In transformative facilitation, the facilitator is not a leader: their
role is to enable the group members to lead themselves. My colleague Betty Sue Flowers said to me:

> I've experienced a lot of bad facilitating where the facili-
> tator was confused about being a leader. This is easy to
> do because you feel like an orchestra conductor trying
> to get the trumpets to pipe down so the violins can rise
> above the din, etc. But the conductor and everyone in the
> orchestra are following a score: it's the composer who's
> really the leader. In the case of the facilitator, it's
> the group that's creating the music in real time. The facili-
> tator "just" has to be able to hear it in all its complex
> parts and movements and amplify it and, in the end, write
> down the score.

When participants are collaborating, they are not forcing,
adapting, or exiting: they have chosen not to boss others around
or to be bossed around. Facilitating collaboration therefore
requires humility. This is a stretch for facilitators who want to be
heroic leaders.

In 2002, I facilitated a large international workshop in Stowe, Vermont. Susan Taylor, a thoughtful and sensitive colleague, attended; we had been working together for years, but she had never seen me facilitating. In our office I was usually placid or grumpy, but she said that at this workshop she saw a different person. "This is the first time I've seen you fully alive!"

What Taylor noticed when she saw me facilitating was partly that, after many years of practice, I had become good at and comfortable with this work, and was able to relax and enjoy the high-wire challenge and spotlight of giving such a live public performance. More fundamentally, it is that this is my vocation: my chosen lifelong way of serving. Serving enables us to escape our small, defensive, egoic self and enact our larger, better, and more alive one, and in doing so to inspire others to do the same.

When I facilitated with O'Brien, he always insisted on having thirty minutes alone just before we started a meeting to collect his thoughts. He told me, "The success of an intervention depends on the interior condition of the intervenor." O'Brien was pointing to the importance of the inner orientation of the facilitator, and especially of a focus on serving with what he called love. "By 'love,'" he wrote, "I mean a predisposition toward helping another person to become complete: to develop to their full potential. Love is not something that suddenly strikes us—it is an act of the will. By 'an act of will,' I mean that you do not have to like someone to love him or her."[1]

I saw the impact of serving in 2019 in Ethiopia. After a long history of authoritarian governments, Prime Minister Abiy Ahmed was attempting to implement major national reforms through releasing political detainees, allowing exiled dissidents and insurgents to return home, and appointing former prisoners of conscience to positions in institutions such as the electoral board. For these actions and for making peace with neighboring Eritrea, he was awarded that year's Nobel Peace Prize. But these upheavals in how things work and who controls what, against a backdrop of deep ethnic, religious, regional, and political tensions, created violence as well as peace: three million Ethiopians were displaced within the country, more than any other country in the world. For Ethiopians to transform their country democratically and sustainably, rather than forcibly and temporarily, they needed to build trust.

That year, the Destiny Ethiopia project convened fifty top national leaders from every major group to contribute to peace and progress. At the conclusion of their second workshop, in July 2019, one team member, an opposition politician, was standing on the front steps of the rural hotel where we had been meeting. In the weeks prior to the event, during an upsurge of deadly political violence, members of his party had been rounded up by the government, so he had been frightened about coming to the workshop and had requested that the meeting organizer arrange for him to travel, disguised, in a convoy guarded by commandos. On that last day of the workshop, the organizer asked the politician if he needed the same arrangements made for his trip back to the capital. The politician gestured toward his government counterpart, who was standing nearby. "No," the politician said, "I'll ride back with him." In many contexts, collaboration requires courage.

The politician made this dramatic shift simply as a result of meeting, observing, and talking with his opponents during the various plenary and small-group activities during the workshop. Such a process for building trust is not complicated, but it is crucial. Lack of trust creates fear, defensiveness, and rigidity. Trust enables openness, fluidity, and a willingness to take risks. All transformations, whether of countries, communities, or companies, require trust. Trust is required to produce contribution, connection, and equity.

In December 2019, the whole Ethiopian team stood on a stage in a hotel ballroom in Addis Ababa, in front of national and international dignitaries and media, broadcasting on live television and the internet, and held hands and read a declaration of the actions they would take, together, to improve the country's future. They had choreographed the event to demonstrate their unity and mutual respect. The welcome was given in five languages and English—not only in Amharic, the national working language and the mother tongue of the second-largest ethnic group. Each part of their report was presented by two politicians from opposing parties, with the presenters chosen by lot in front of the audience. Each of the team members spoke briefly about what the project had meant for them. The common theme across all of their testimonials was, "I thought that it would be impossible for us to work together, but I discovered that it is possible."

Afterward members of the team appeared together in television, radio, and conference interviews and panels; they even competed together on a game show. The whole country saw a radically different way of engaging with complex challenges than they were used to: their leaders were being thoughtful, respectful, relaxed, and open with people they were in conflict with. The efforts of this team were not sufficient to produce peace throughout the country, and in 2020 violent conflict broke out again in the north. But the team demonstrated what it takes to build trust and peace.

The project facilitation team succeeded in organizing a process within which participants chose to make such extraordinary, coordinated, consequential actions, primarily because we served them. In late 2017, I had started corresponding about the possibility of such a project with a young Ethiopian professional named Negusu Aklilu, and six months later I met with him and two of his friends to discuss the initiative. I liked them and wanted to help, but doubted whether they had the capacity to get the project off the ground. I thought that they weren't powerful or connected enough to be able to convene political and social leaders from across the fractured Ethiopian landscape. I couldn't see how they would be able to get the support they would need to undertake a collaboration that could make a difference.

Yet by mid-2019, Negusu and his colleagues had succeeded in putting together a team of unprecedented influence and diversity. They had done this simply by having meeting after meeting, over months and months, explaining what they were trying to do and gradually enrolling the people they needed. The source of their impressive success was obvious to everyone who met them: they had a novel proposal that made sense in the national context, they were acting not primarily for their personal benefit but for the benefit of the country, and they kept at it doggedly and courageously. The people they met saw them as ordinary citizens with extraordinary character and commitment to serve.

Negusu's facilitation focused on cultivating the participation of the leaders in the work of the project. They each had their own personal and political idiosyncrasies and needs, and many of them were demanding and hard to keep on board, but Negusu treated them all with respect and love. He was content to delegate other tasks to other members of our facilitation team. In the first planning meeting of our full team, he didn't say much until I asked him for his views on team norms, and he replied firmly that he could live with any of our foibles except actions that endangered the project. During the workshops, in our twice-daily facilitation team meetings, Negusu kept reminding us to provide the participants with "Cloud 9 service." (This is the slogan of Ethiopian Airlines' VIP frequent flyer club.)

Negusu's focus on serving the participants enabled the project's success. The context of the project was unstable and dangerous, so the participants were slow to trust one another and our facilitation team. Initially many were concerned that Negusu and his colleagues might have a hidden partisan agenda, but as the project continued, most of them concluded that his and our intention was simply to serve them, and through them the project and the country.

It was this trust of the participants in the intention of the facilitation team that enabled us to move fluidly between directing and accompanying. Many times, in running particular project activities, such as the stakeholder workshops, we were directive in setting objectives, methodology, pace, and ground rules—behaving like a strict orchestra director. At other times, such as when implementing activities for the participants to engage with their own diverse constituencies, we followed along behind, cultivating the emerging energy of the participants—acting like a diligent accompanying pianist. We did not push the river, nor did we just let it flow: we worked energetically and attentively to remove the obstacles to its flow.

Negusu's sincere, humble orientation to serve set the tone for our facilitation team and for the project. He described our role as doing the "professional, technical, donkey work" to maintain the integrity of the project. We faced lots of complications and challenges, but mostly without the competitive egoic battles that so often sink collaborations. I trusted Negusu and was inspired by his example, and played my facilitation role more humbly than usual and with less need to assert and control.

A facilitator cannot make participants do anything, yet it is not enough for the facilitator just to follow behind what participants are choosing to do. The facilitator's job is to help participants choose and coordinate their actions so that they can move forward together. Roger Fisher, the author of the negotiating bible *Getting to Yes*, once advised me, "Don't be trusting; be trustworthy." In transformative facilitation, the facilitator and participants cycle back and forth between *directing* and *accompanying*, over and over as needed. This requires genuine, humble, trustworthy *serving*.

10

How Do We Understand Our Role?
Standing Outside and Inside

*T*ransformative facilitation is a process in which participants and facilitators work together to transform a problematic situation. The fifth and most fundamental question they need to work with is: How do we understand our roles and responsibilities?

In vertical facilitation, participants see the situation they are facing as problematic, and they are collaborating in order to address it. They approach the situation as if they were *outside* (apart from) it, saying "We must fix it." Facilitators also position themselves outside: they see their role as helping the participants change what they are doing so that the situation can change. The upside of this approach is objectivity. The downside of overemphasizing this approach, without making room for personal responsibility, is that it produces coldness and abdication: the arrogant view that for the situation to change, *other* people must change.

In horizontal facilitation, participants see themselves as *inside* (part of) the situation. They are collaborating because they see themselves as partly responsible for things being as they are and therefore partly responsible for changing the way things are. They say, "We must each put our own house in order." The facilitator understands that in playing their own role in the group, they are also partly responsible for what is happening. The upside of this approach is self-reflectivity and self-responsibility. The downside of overemphasizing this approach, without making room for an outside-in view, is that it produces myopia: people getting so caught up with their personal dynamics that they lose sight of the larger systemic dynamics of the situation.

Here again, transformative facilitation cycles between two poles to get the best of both and avoid the worst. The facilitator positions themself as both outside *and* inside the group and the situation, and thereby helps the participants do the same. To be able to cycle between these two outer moves, the inner shift required of the facilitator—the specific way of paying attention—is *partnering*.

The fifth and most fundamental choice required of the facilitator, then, moment to moment and over and over, is this: Do I focus on standing outside or on standing inside?

THE FACILITATOR STANDS IN TWO WORLDS

I thought that we had prepared the first workshop perfectly. Eight months before, in March 2018, I had received an email from Melanie MacKinnon, a member of Misipawistik Cree Nation and executive director of Ongomiizwin Indigenous Institute of Health and Healing at the University of Manitoba in Canada. MacKinnon has spent her career working in First Nations (Native Canadian) health, and now she saw an opening to contribute to making things better.

On the one hand, systemic anti-Indigenous racism was producing worsening health outcomes for First Nations people in Manitoba. Their life expectancy was eleven years less than that of other Manitobans, whereas in 2002 it had been seven years less. On the other hand, the political context was promising: the three main First Nations political organizations in Manitoba had agreed to work together on health, and the Canadian federal government was open to legislative reforms to give First Nations more authority in this domain. Furthermore, many Manitoba First Nations were getting stronger economically, professionally, and spiritually. A group of Indigenous elders, convened by David Courchene Jr. of the Turtle Lodge Central House of Knowledge, was rearticulating and reasserting traditional, sovereign ways of being and of working with such situations ("We must each put our own house in order"). MacKinnon had just been appointed as an advisor to Arlen Dumas, the grand chief of the Assembly of Manitoba Chiefs, and with his official endorsement was launching an ambitious project to transform the Manitoba First Nations health system.

MacKinnon understood the systemic obstacles to contribution, connection, and equity, including deeply rooted political, economic, institutional, and cultural differences, both among First Nations and between them and Canadians. Her idea was to convene a diverse team of First Nations leaders to create movement toward *mino pimatisiwin* ("the good life" in Cree). She also wanted to create a new braided methodology, one that synthesized the approaches to addressing complex challenges used by First Nations with those used by Reos Partners.[1] I was thrilled to be able to apply what I had learned around the world back in my home country to contribute to solving such an important problem. (South Africa's apartheid system of racial separation and oppression had been modeled on Canada's system of First Nations reserves.) Ten years earlier, I had started to work on a similar project with First Nations in British Columbia that had been initiated by a civil servant in the federal government, but that had not worked out, and I was keen to try again with a project that was initiated and governed by First Nations.

We formed a facilitation team of six professionals from different local First Nations organizations plus five from Reos. Together we designed a process to work first with a team of elders and knowledge keepers (including Courchene and members of his group), chiefs, youth, and professionals working in health, education, and social services, and then with provincial and federal government politicians and officials. Now it was November, and we were ready to start the team's first workshop, at a small hotel on the shore of frozen Lake Winnipeg. I felt confident that our political and professional partnership meant that we were well positioned to do this work, and that after all of my years of facilitating such processes, I now knew what to do.

I was wrong.

We started the workshop with Reos's best tried-and-tested methods, and the participants pushed back immediately. We asked each person to introduce themselves in one minute (which in Mexico had been the crucial symbol of equity), but many participants, especially the elders, were offended when we interrupted them by ringing a bell, with its echoes of the bells rung in the abusive residential schools to which First Nations children had been sent. We introduced the four modes of talking and listening in pairs, including the exercise of partners looking into each other's eyes in the presencing mode (which in Colombia had been so moving), but Courchene and some of the others found this culturally inappropriate. We invited everyone to present an object that for them represented the current reality of the lives of First Nations in Manitoba (which in the drug project had produced a rich picture of contrasting perspectives), but some of them found this triggering of traumatic experiences.

Then I started to make a presentation of the methodology we would be using, as I had often done before, to establish my credibility with examples from previous projects elsewhere. George Muswaggon, a former grand chief from Cross Lake First Nation, spoke up in a calm, matter-of-fact voice: "I don't trust you."

I felt frightened. Twice before in my career, workshop participants had rejected me as a facilitator and asked me to leave their workshops. I had found these experiences humiliating, and I didn't want to be ejected from this project, which I was expecting would make a good contribution to Manitoba and to my and Reos's reputation and income. Between my overconfidence in my facilitation skills and my fear of failing, my orientation toward open-hearted service (which Bill O'Brien had emphasized) was at risk of being eclipsed.

Now I was fully paying attention. I thought I understood why Muswaggon, Courchene, and others in the group didn't trust me and didn't want to go along with the process the facilitation team and I were proposing. I grasped that they were not—as many facilitators lazily assume—"just being difficult." For centuries in Canada (as in other places), Indigenous people have been colonized, massacred, oppressed, marginalized, and cheated by white people, who had arrogantly imposed their way of doing things. The participants in this workshop thought that I was reproducing this vertical "I have the right answer" approach and weren't prepared to accept it. They wanted this process to be run in a way that fit their situation and their way of doing things.

I stumbled through the rest of my presentation, and when I finished, MacKinnon asked Muswaggon whether he trusted me now. He replied, "No, but I trust the process." At that moment I saw clearly what I needed to do. "I am not asking you to trust me or the process," I said. "I am suggesting that we just take the next step and then see where we are and what we want to do next." He agreed, and we continued. With this partnering statement, I moved from being apart from the group toward also being a part.

A little while later, we took a break in the meeting. The participants went to the room next door to have coffee, and the facilitation team huddled around a table in the meeting room. We were all upset that the participants had rejected our process. The First Nations facilitators felt offended that their understanding of First Nations teachings and practices and their role in designing this innovative process had not been recognized by the participants. I felt underappreciated and wanted to quit.

But within fifteen minutes, we had decided to pivot sharply. When the meeting resumed, we took a different approach that reduced the dominance of the Reos methodology: starting and ending every day in traditional spiritual ceremony led by Courchene and others; fewer, shorter structured activities; more of the facilitation done by the First Nations members of our team and less by Reos; and a parallel track of a self-facilitated conversation among the elders. By the third day of the workshop, I had shifted into a more unmistakably humble position: I didn't say a word in the workshop sessions, supporting the group from the sidelines and focusing on serving snacks and picking up dirty plates and coffee cups. That day was my birthday, and after the ceremony Courchene wished me well, and Muswaggon gave me a gift of a sacred object. I was forgiven for the error I had made by standing outside and above.

When I had advocated that we use activities that had worked in other contexts (downloading my previously formed theories and practices), I was not paying adequate attention to the particular situation we were facing in that place at that time. But after Muswaggon's statement, the whole facilitation team saw more clearly this situation, which enabled us to pivot successfully. Transformative facilitation involves studying and practicing frameworks like the ones in this book, and then suspending them to pay attention to the situation that is in front of us.

—————

Our new, more tightly braided approach worked better, and over the months that followed, the project advanced.[2] Our facilitation team succeeded in working with the first four polarities:

1. Advocating for the processes that we thought, based on our experience, would work best, and also inquiring after the feedback of the participants and then incorporating it

2. Reaching agreements to deliver on project milestones and also continuing to advance through continued nonagreement

3. Mapping out a project path and also pivoting as we discovered what we needed to do next

4. Directing the project as a whole and also accompanying the participants as they each dealt with their own particular imperatives and constraints

The key to our facilitation team's ability to manage these four polarities was our being able to manage a fifth, more fundamental one: being *apart* and being *a part*. The members of our team came from both outside and inside Manitoba First Nations, and we were therefore able to bring both sets of experiences and perspectives to our work. The complex dynamics in the larger system—including the struggles for recognition, resources, and self-realization, among First Nations and between First Nations and Canadians—also showed up within our team. Marcia Anderson, a Cree-Anishinaabe member of our facilitation team, reminded us of the words of Black civil rights activist Audre Lorde, "The master's tools will never dismantle the master's house."[3] My tools from outside would never be sufficient to remove the obstacles to First Nations' contribution, connection, and equity.

But we didn't give up. Our awareness of and attention to these dynamics, sometimes painful and sometimes playful, enabled us to make our way forward together and help the participants do the same. This partnership among the First Nations and Reos members of the facilitation team was essential to the project's success.

I felt the tension of this fifth polarity, especially from the moment Muswaggon said he didn't trust me. On the one hand, I saw myself as apart from the Manitoba First Nations situation: I was not from Manitoba or a First Nation and was seen by them as an outsider; I had been hired as an external expert on the basis of my independence and international experience; and I was content (even smugly superior) with this positioning and to have been asked by MacKinnon and Dumas to help them. On the other hand, as Muswaggon and other participants had made clear, I was not simply a neutral outsider, but a part of the Canadian system that they found problematic. (It was now I who was being referred to as a settler, as the white participants had been at Mont Fleur in South Africa.) But because I and the facilitation team grasped and were willing to live with this permanent tension, as partners, we were able to keep our footing and move forward.

Muswaggon and I also found some opportunities to talk over several meals. Given what he had said at the first meeting, I was surprised at his kindness toward me. "The history of my people means that we cannot dole out trust like candy," he told me. "But I observed you and prayed and decided that you are a good person. This trust is simple and will last."

STANDING OUTSIDE IS VALUABLE

The conventional stance of a facilitator is to stand apart from the situation and the participants, trying to be attentive and supportive, but clear that the responsibility and risk for the situation and for efforts to change it rest with the participants. The facilitator is a neutral referee, sometimes helpful to the group's being able to make progress, and sometimes a minor and quickly forgotten figure. For most facilitators this is a comfortable default positioning.

It can be useful for the facilitator to stand apart and be able to observe and contribute to the situation and the group from outside. From my first experience in South Africa to this one in Manitoba, my position as a less involved and more objective outsider has enabled me to support groups of participants who all have a stake in and history with the situation and need to stand back to see it afresh. Most of the time, I am able to stay calm and curious, without getting bated or hooked, even in contexts that are swirling with anger and fear.

A facilitator who is standing apart can help the participants see their situation with greater distance and dispassion. Leadership scholars Ronald Heifetz and Marty Linsky write:

> The ability to maintain perspective in the midst of action
> is critical to lowering resistance. Any military officer

knows the importance of maintaining the capacity for reflection, especially in the "fog of war." Great athletes must simultaneously play the game and observe it as a whole. We call this skill "getting off the dance floor and going to the balcony," an image that captures the mental activity of stepping back from the action and asking, "What's really going on here?"[4]

In Reos projects, one way we help a group of stakeholders go to the balcony is to talk with each of them individually in advance of their first meeting and then to send them a report containing an organized list of verbatim, unattributed quotes from the statements they made. Then, at the first meeting we ask them to study and discuss this document objectively, from the outside, as if the text contained statements by other people. Going to the balcony is a way of suspending one's position and perspective.

Another way to go to the balcony is for participants and facilitators to watch for ways in which dynamics in the larger situation they are working with (the macrocosm) are showing up within their own group (the microcosm). In Manitoba, I got my clearest view of the larger First Nations–Canadian dynamics by paying attention to how these were manifesting within our facilitation team. The practice of standing apart can make a crucial contribution to understanding what is happening in the situation and how to transform it.

STANDING INSIDE IS VALUABLE

Standing apart from the problematic situation is useful, but so is the opposite and more challenging positioning: acknowledging and acting from one's role as a part of the situation. Boston College leadership professor Bill Torbert once said to me, "The 1960s slogan 'If you're not part of the solution, you're part of the problem' misses the crucial point, which is that if you're not part of the problem, you can't be part of the solution." If you can't see the ways in which what you are doing or not doing is contributing to producing the problematic situation, then you cannot contribute to changing that situation, except from outside. This stance of being outside and above often produces condescension and imposition and hence countervailing resistance and mistrust, as it did in the dynamics between me and the group during the first day of the Manitoba workshop. Such verticality ("We have the right answer") generates defensive horizontality ("We each have our own answer").

Many facilitators position themselves as outside. They are working on the situation rather than as part of it, like the person who telephones home from their car and says, "I am in traffic" rather than "I am traffic." This positioning of being apart limits the ways they are able to contribute to changing the situation: they can only advise (like a consultant) or force (like a boss). If they want to contribute as a collaborator, then they need also to recognize and take responsibility for the roles and actions they are currently taking or not taking that are contributing to the situation being as it is. This more humble dual positioning enables the facilitator to have more influence.

For people who are used to positioning themselves, politically or psychologically, as outside and above ("I am innocent"), such taking of responsibility ("I am not innocent") involves an uncomfortable stretch. A crucial challenge in trying to effect transformation through collaboration is therefore to be able to see how one is part of the problematic situation.

In 2006, I facilitated an ambitious and complex multi-stakeholder collaboration in India to reduce child malnutrition. At one point, the project became so complicated and confusing that I went to a local colleague, Arun Maira, and asked him to explain to me what we were really doing. "You have to remember," he replied, "that most of the time when a group of stakeholder leaders gets together to work on a problem, every one of them believes that if only the other ones would change what they are thinking and doing, then the problem would be solved. But if all the participants are involved, then it can't all be the fault of others! The real innovation here is that we are inviting these leaders to reflect on how they might need to change what they themselves are doing."

Some years ago, I cofacilitated several times with a Paraguayan colleague named Jorge Talavera. My Spanish was not good and neither was his English, so we limited our workshop conversations to essential matters. One dynamic we thought was essential was what we called *el click*: that moment in a workshop when a participant realizes that for the problematic situation they are working on to change, they themself would need to change.

This crucial click is less common for the facilitator than for participants. The role of the facilitator in a situation is usually more distant and less obvious than for a stakeholder. But however small or large this role is, the facilitator must acknowledge it. On the first day of the Manitoba workshop, Muswaggon's statement helped me make such a click from seeing myself as apart from the First Nations–Canadian situation to also recognizing myself as a part of it. Such clicks of switching between standing outside and standing inside are required for transformative facilitation.

When someone shows us something about ourselves that we had not seen and do not like, we usually recoil in discomfort and denial. When I first started working with MacKinnon, she invited me to attend and speak at a First Nations health conference in Winnipeg. As I sat in the audience with her and her colleagues and listened to the presentation of a white federal government official, and then to Dumas criticizing that official's arrogance, I was happy to be on the side of the good guys. Later, when Muswaggon said that he didn't trust me, I felt afraid, but I was able to hear him. This encounter, which at the same time felt both confrontational and embracing, enabled me to see more clearly what I was doing and to change it.

My colleague Ian Prinsloo introduced an exercise into our workshops to help participants explore moving back and forth between being apart and being a part. We ask them to write two one-page essays about the problematic situation they are dealing with. In the first essay, they describe the situation as if they were observing or directing it from the outside, writing down in detail what other people are doing that is contributing to the situation's being as it is and what those people need to do differently to enable the situation to get unstuck and move forward. In the second essay, they describe this same situation as if they themselves were participating in and cocreating it from the inside, writing down in detail what they are doing that is contributing to the situation's being as it is and what they need to do differently to enable the situation to get unstuck and move forward.

When we then ask the participants what differences they noticed in themselves in shifting from the first (outside) stance to the second (inside) one, they typically make two observations. In the second essay, they felt more guilty and burdened, and also thought they had more options as to actions they could take and more energy to act. Standing inside produces both more responsibility and more agency.

Another simple and powerful activity we often do in workshops is to invite participants to pair up with someone in the group who they think is most different from them and to go for a thirty-minute walk together. The first time I did this was in 1998 in Guatemala; the country had just agreed on a set of peace accords to end the long, genocidal civil war, and I was facilitating a workshop on how to implement these accords.

Hugo Beteta, a foundation executive, and Otilia Lux de Coti, an Indigenous human rights campaigner, took this walk together. They were an unlikely pair, from two realities separated politically, economically, socially, and culturally (as in Canada). I was sitting in the meeting room, waiting for the participants to return, when Beteta entered looking stunned. I asked him what had happened. "Otilia told me a story about her high school graduation that really shook me up," he replied. "She'd received the highest grades of any graduating student and was given the honor of carrying the national flag onto the stage, but the school wouldn't allow her to wear her traditional ethnic clothing to the ceremony. So she was forced to choose between having her accomplishment recognized and offending her family and betraying herself. I hadn't grasped how we Guatemalans have built everyday mechanisms for perpetuating the racism and inequality that produced the genocide." Lux de Coti showed Beteta how their situation looked from her perspective, and he recognized his responsibility in this situation and what he needed to do to change it. Later, Lux de Coti became minister of culture and Beteta minister of finance, and they worked together to increase Indigenous inclusion in Guatemala.

This paired-walk exercise is simple, yet it's one of the exercises that workshop participants say has the biggest impact on their understanding of their situation and their relationships with others. Why is this simple activity so fruitful?

On one level, the walk is effective because of its mechanics. Two people who are curious to connect move forward side by side (or, if they aren't able or don't want to walk, sit side by side)—relaxed and in nature, looking at the world together—and talk informally, without papers, phones, or other distractions, dealing together with whatever arises on their short journey. The walk offers them an opportunity within the structured context of the workshop to connect on a human level, as equals, and to share their perspectives. This experience can produce profound changes. Almost everyone who has gone on these walks over the years says that, like Beteta, they were surprised and affected to see the world through the eyes of their partners, with whom they expected to have nothing in common.

Lucila Servitje, a Catholic theologian who participated in this activity at a Possible Mexicos workshop, offered me a deeper explanation for why it's effective. She suggested that the walk and the private informal sharing of stories have an impact because they involve mutual acceptance, and this feeling of being accepted is what enables the participants to change their thinking and actions. The sequence here—first a person is accepted and then they reconsider their position—is the opposite of the traditional Catholic confession, where first a person confesses and then they're forgiven. The walk, she says, is like God's grace: love we receive that we don't have to earn. My colleague Brenna Atnikov says that in our work in Manitoba, our First Nations partners showed us such grace, and this helped us do more fluidly what was needed of us.

———

The strongest spur to people changing what they're doing is not so much seeing their situation differently as seeing themselves differently. This sort of shift in self-perception often comes about through confrontations and challenges that are unsettling and show us that we're not as we thought we were. In the story of the Possible Mexicos banker who confronted the chairman of the company that had interviewed the transgender woman, the chairman was embarrassed by what he realized that he, as the leader of that organization, was doing, and this motivated him to change. Most people, when they see that what they are doing is unjust—when they are able to step back from the fray, go to the balcony, and see the larger picture of what is happening and their role in it—feel responsible to change. Inviting participants to ask themselves the self-reflective question, "In this situation, what is my role and my responsibility?" can provoke and inspire them to alter what they're doing. This approach can lead to transformation—not forcefully from outside and above, but freely from within.

At the 2017 workshop in Colombia, Francisco de Roux told me a story about how he too had been confronted with his role and responsibility. He had gone into the jungle to negotiate with a guerilla leader whose unit was detaining some civilians. He started this conversation, as he usually did, by saying, "I don't understand why you are doing this, but I assume you are doing it for the good of the country, as I am. How does this work ethically?" I interpreted de Roux's position as having been respectful and apart, as if to say, "I am not involved in this situation, but I want to help you do the right thing." But then, de Roux told me, the guerilla asked, "Haven't you Jesuits been involved for generations in running universities that educate the elite? So don't you have some responsibility for what the elite have been doing in this country?" De Roux said that this unexpected challenge provoked him to see a way in which he was part of the problematic situation he was trying to address, and therefore that in his work as a peacemaker, he needed to engage not just with marginalized participants but also with privileged ones (as he was doing at our workshop).

THE KEY TO COMBINING STANDING OUTSIDE AND INSIDE IS PARTNERING

"In a ham omelet," the quip goes, "the chicken is involved but the pig is committed." Facilitators who insist that their role in a collaboration is only that of a chicken—that they are merely advisers, helpers, or consultants, and so have limited responsibility and accountability—will have limited influence. Those who want more influence must be pigs as well as chickens.

Like the four pairs of moves described in the previous four chapters, standing outside and inside is a polarity, not a choice, and holding both positions is embracing a paradox (a mystery) that we can appreciate but cannot solve. Psychologist Robert

Johnson suggests the medieval Christian image of the mandorla as a means to effect such reconciliation:

> A mandorla is that almond-shaped segment that is made when two circles partly overlap. This symbol signifies nothing less than the overlap of the opposites that we have been investigating. The mandorla instructs us how to engage in reconciliation. It begins the healing of the split. The overlap generally is very tiny at first, only a sliver of the new moon; but it is a beginning. As time passes, the greater the overlap, the greater and more complete is the healing. The mandorla binds together that which was torn apart and made unwhole—unholy.[5]

We learn to be both apart and a part through gradually becoming more conscious of and present to both poles and allowing them to overlap and the split between them to heal.

The orientation required for this reconciliation is *partnering*. My longest experience of partnering is my thirty years of being married to Dorothy. Being married offers the partners the opportunity to become more fully united and therefore one, and at the same time for each of them to become more fully themselves and therefore two: a part and also apart. Over this same period, I have also been a coowner of Reos Partners and its predecessor companies (for much of this time, partnerships in the legal sense), so I know how partnering produces both opportunities and obligations. Not all collaborations require such deep and long commitment: my work with the Manitoba team lasted for only eighteen months.

In transformative facilitation, the facilitator and participants cycle back and forth between *standing outside*, on the balcony, and *standing inside*, assuming their responsibilities for the situation being as it is and for what this implies for what they need to do about it. This requires *partnering*.

Conclusion

Removing the Obstacles
to Love, Power, and Justice

*T*ransformative facilitation helps people who are facing a problematic situation collaborate to transform that situation. Collaboration offers a crucial multilateral alternative to unilateral forcing, adapting, and exiting.

The stories I have told in the preceding chapters explain how transformative facilitation helps groups break through from stuckness to flow and thereby to move forward together. *Move* means not only to talk but also to act. *Forward* means acting not simply to reproduce the status quo but to make things better. And *together* means acting not only each in one's own way but with some degree of alignment.

Transformative facilitation therefore offers a possibility that is larger than only helping groups address their particular situations. It offers a way to escape from the twin dangers of imposition and fragmentation. Transformative facilitation offers a way to create a better world.

Transformative facilitation
TRANSFORMS PROBLEMATIC SITUATIONS

I have often seen the breakthrough from stuckness to flow in the work of groups who are dealing with everyday challenges and conflicts within their organization and with their organization's work in the world. I have also often seen it in the work of cross-organizational groups who are dealing with societal challenges and conflicts. These experiences have given me clear pictures of the before and after of transformative facilitation.

In November 2019, I saw a clear "before" picture of stuckness. I had just arrived in Port-au-Prince, the capital of Haiti. Jean Paul Faubert, a local businessman, had picked me up at the airport to drive me to my hotel for us to begin a week of meetings about a national collaboration that we and others were organizing. The city had been shut down for six months by protests against disastrous corruption and violence—an extreme version of situations that occur in many countries. In Haitian Creole, this stuck situation was called *peyi lok*: country lockdown.

I found our one-hour drive terrifying. Over and over, we found the street in front of us blocked by protestors or a barricade or burning garbage. We had to keep stopping, asking questions of the protestors and a security adviser we had on the phone, and turning to find a new way forward. Finally, we got to the hotel, where we immediately began a series of thoughtful, warm, energetic conversations with people who wanted to transform this situation. (Afterwards these people enrolled others, and this larger group collaborated to effect such a national transformation, including in the workshop I described in chapter 9.)

This is the starting point for all transformative facilitation. A group of people find the situation that they are facing to be problematic. They and others may have attempted to deal with it through forcing, adapting, and exiting, but have found that these options have been inadequate and have produced stuckness. They want to collaborate to find a better way forward.

In February 2018, in Mexico, I saw an equally clear "after" picture of a group in flow (six months after that group had started off stuck). A Possible Mexicos team had been working hard all day, arguing and laughing, and were advancing well in their work. One of the facilitators said, awestruck, "This is heaven on earth!" At dinner, participant Lucila Servitje and I talked about what we were seeing that might merit such an exalted description: everyone being able to bring all of themselves to the work, to be embraced as fellow humans, and to participate in doing something worthwhile together that none of them could do alone.

That day was a sweet moment of progress. Before and after, we also had sour moments of stuckness. Collaborating in diverse teams to work on problematic situations always involves ups and downs. But this experience of "heaven on earth" proved to us that it is possible, not only in theory but in practice, to move forward together: that even if this movement is not necessarily easy or programmable or sufficient, it is possible. Success in such contexts is never guaranteed, but transformative facilitation makes it more likely.

TRANSFORMATIVE FACILITATION EMPLOYS LOVE, POWER, AND JUSTICE

The participants in Possible Mexicos refer to their project as a "living example" of a better country. In the midst of so many daunting challenges and ineffective responses, there and elsewhere, providing this example has been one of their most important contributions to creating a better future. In this case and the others in this book, the facilitation team helped the group move from stuckness to flow by helping them remove obstacles to contribution, connection, and equity.

But there is a more fundamental and expansive way to express this core strategy of transformative facilitation: it helps people remove the obstacles to love, power, and justice. This latter formulation extends and corrects an omission in my previous writing about facilitating change, which focused only on the first two elements, love and power.[1] The third element, justice, is required if facilitation is not merely to rearrange the status quo but to effect systemic transformation.

The words *love, power,* and *justice* have weighty political, philosophical, and moral connotations. They are used in many different ways and are thus heavily freighted. Nevertheless, I use them because, when defined clearly, they provide a profound and precise way to understand and employ transformative facilitation.

Love is the drive toward unity that in a collaboration manifests as connections among the participants and between them and their situation. Power is the drive toward self-realization that manifests as the contributions that the participants make to their collaborative work and to their situation. Justice is the structure that enables and directs love and power and that manifests as equity within the group and, through their work, in the situation.

To understand what it means in practice for a facilitator to help participants enable love and connection, power and contribution, and justice and equity, consider the everyday cases of a facilitator disabling them—of putting in place structural obstacles rather than removing them—and of examples of processes that can contribute to enabling them.

A facilitator obstructs *love and connection* when they organize a process so formally that it leaves few openings for participants to engage fully with one another and with the larger situation. In this case, the participants will complain of insufficient creativity, because new ideas most often come from new connections. ("Your process is not producing anything new!") One simple archetypal example of a process for enabling love is the paired walk (as described in chapter 10), in that it enables two people to connect as fellow humans and to reflect on the roles they are playing in their situation. Another example is grouping ideas written on sticky notes, in that doing so enables each person to see how their ideas relate to those of others.

A facilitator disables or obstructs *power and contribution* when they organize a process so tightly that participants are unable to express themselves. In this case, the participants will complain that they are being prevented from participating fully in the work. ("You're cutting us off!") One example of a process for enabling power is Open Space Technology, in that its basic invitation is for participants to choose a working group for which they have the most energy and that provides them a focused opportunity to work on something that matters to them, rather than engaging in a disempowering process of everyone working on everything. Another example is peer coaching, where participants take turns helping one another find more effective ways to implement the action plans for which they are responsible.

A facilitator obstructs *justice and equity* when they organize a process in a way that allows the power of some participants to dominate that of others. In this case, the participants will complain that they are being treated unfairly, often in a way that mirrors unfairness in the larger system. ("You're favoring the boss!") One example of a process for enabling justice is to intentionally compose a collaboration to include participants who are usually ignored or marginalized. Another example is for participants and facilitators to pay attention to and talk about how their own team dynamics are reproducing injustices in the larger system; they then have the opportunity to change these dynamics and enable all participants to contribute and connect equitably.

Transformative facilitation enables people to move forward together by engaging all three of these generative drives. (The three words *move forward together* refer to the drives of power, justice, and love, respectively.) Just like the vertical-horizontal polarities explored in the previous chapters, love, power, and justice are in permanent creative tension. I experience this tension not only when I facilitate in client groups but also when I facilitate as a manager in Reos: I have to find a way to engage each person's gifts and growth (including my own) *and* help people work together as a team *and* make the organization more just.

It can seem straightforward to enable and balance the drives of power, love, and justice when you read about them in a book or work with them in a relaxed setting. But under the tension and stress of high complexity and low control, most people contract to their comfort zone and favor one or two of these drives. A facilitator must continuously attend to rebalancing and in particular to strengthening their own weaker drives.

This is the tango of transformative facilitation. The facilitators and participants attentively employ the five sets of paired moves and five shifts, as and when needed, moving back and forth between vertical and horizontal, wholes and parts, power and love, by turns slow and fast, in balance and off balance. They engage power when they contribute and grow. They engage love when they connect and unite. They engage justice to provide their movement with purpose, direction, and structure.

Transformative facilitation enables the threefold transformative potential of love, power, and justice. I think this is what Francisco de Roux was pointing me toward when he observed, "You are removing the obstacles to the expression of the mystery!"

LOVE IS THE DRIVE TO UNITE THE SEPARATED

In my first book, *Solving Tough Problems,* I told a story of a minute of silence in the 1998 workshop in Guatemala that I referred to in chapter 10.[2] Since 1960, the right-wing government of Guatemala had fought a civil war against left-wing rebels. The United Nations–sponsored investigation of the war concluded that the government's deliberate and systematic destruction of Indigenous communities constituted genocide. In 1996, the warring parties had signed a set of peace accords. The workshop I facilitated was the beginning of a project that brought together leaders from across the deep divisions of Guatemalan society—cabinet ministers, former army and guerrilla officers, businessmen, journalists, youth, Indigenous people—to develop pathways to implement the accords.

The participants in the workshop had been on different sides of the war, so the room was thick with suspicion. One morning in a storytelling circle, Ronalth Ochaeta, a human rights investigator for the Catholic Church, related his experience of having gone to an Indigenous village to observe the exhumation of a mass grave from a wartime massacre. When the earth had been removed from the grave, Ochaeta noticed lots of small bones and asked the forensic scientist supervising the exhumation what had happened. The scientist replied that the massacre had included pregnant women, and the small bones were of their fetuses.

After Ochaeta told this story in our workshop, the room fell completely silent for a long time. Then the team took a break and afterward continued with their work. In the years that followed, they collaborated on many national initiatives, including four presidential campaigns; contributions to the Commission for Historical Clarification, the Fiscal Agreement Commission, and the Peace Accords Monitoring Commission; work on municipal development strategies, a national antipoverty strategy, and a new university curriculum; and six spin-off national dialogues.

In 2000, when Katrin Kaeufer of MIT led a research project that interviewed the team, several of them referred to this minute of silence to explain how they had been inspired to come together to accomplish what they had. One of them said, "In giving his testimony, Ochaeta was sincere, calm, and serene, without a trace of hate in his voice. This gave way to the moment of silence that, I would say, lasted at least one minute. It was horrible! It was a very moving experience for all of us. If you ask any of us, we would say that this moment was like a large communion." Another said, "After listening to Ochaeta's story, I understood and felt in my heart all that had happened. And there was a feeling that we must struggle to prevent this from happening again."[3] Ochaeta's story enabled the team to connect deeply to one another, to their situation, and to what they needed to do.

This incident in Guatemala amazed me and was at the center of my early theorizing about facilitation. I interpreted the silence that followed Ochaeta's story as exemplifying not merely connection but communion or love. Here I was using the definition of love given by Protestant theologian Paul Tillich: "the drive towards the unity of the separated."[4] Love in this sense is the universal drive not simply to connect but to make whole that which has become or appears fragmented. I employed this definition of love—there are many I could have used—because it expressed precisely the experience I had had, in Guatemala and elsewhere, that transformative facilitation involves bringing together participants and the parts of the system they represent to act with unity (more precisely, to enact a unity that had always been present but had been obscured).

In the workshop in Guatemala, love was the drive of the leaders to re-knit a national social fabric that had been violently torn. In everyday collaborations, love is the drive of team members to work together and in alignment rather than separately and at cross-purposes. Transformative facilitation removes obstacles to love.

For the facilitator to be able to help unblock love in the work of a group, the facilitator has to be able to unblock it within themself. I experience this drive toward the unity of the separated as a longing to find my part in larger wholes. This is why my experience at Mont Fleur—of discovering a vocation that gave me a useful way to employ my gifts, of having a role in the momentous transformation in South Africa, of connecting warmly with the participants, and of meeting Dorothy—felt like cracking open. This experience and later ones, including the silence in Guatemala, reinforced for me the importance of opening myself up to support the opening up of others. My demeanor as a facilitator is usually reserved and analytical, but many of the times I have been most helpful to a group have been when I have revealed my emotions (excited, touched, or worried) or relaxed into the work (moving in flow, making jokes, creating moments of silence or song). A facilitator has to connect to be able to support participants to connect.

POWER IS THE DRIVE TO SELF-REALIZATION

One of the members of the Guatemala team I became friends with was Clara Arenas, a researcher and activist who during the war had acted courageously to support endangered communities. When I visited her in Guatemala City in 2008, ten years after the first workshop, she challenged the emphasis I had been giving in my writing to dialogue, unity, and love. "Do you know," she asked me, "that last week, the coalition of civil society organizations I am part of took out a full-page advertisement in the main newspaper here, saying that we would no longer participate in dialogues with the government? The government has said that a precondition for us participating in their dialogues is that we refrain from marching and demonstrating in the streets. But these actions are the main way we mobilize and manifest our power, and if dialoguing requires us to surrender our power, then we are not interested."

This conversation with Arenas prompted me to enlarge my theory to take into account not only love but also power. Here again I found that Tillich's framework expressed precisely the phenomenon I was trying to make sense of. He defines power as "the drive of everything living to realize itself, with increasing intensity and extensity."[5] So power in this sense is the universal drive not simply to contribute but to achieve one's purpose and grow. Facilitation must involve helping participants not only unite but also express their needs and find a way forward that gets these needs met.

In Arenas's story, power was the drive of both the government and the civil society organizations to assert and defend their interests. In everyday collaborations, it is the drive of all team members to act to fulfill their agendas and ambitions. Transformative facilitation removes obstacles to power.

The three-part thesis of my second book, *Power and Love*, therefore became the following. First, power, when exercised in a way that denies connection and love (the parts ignoring the larger whole), becomes degenerative power-over. In a couple, for example, power denying love is manifested by the person who is so focused on their own work and career that they neglect their connection to their partner. In an organization, it is a person acting to achieve their objectives in a way that ignores their impact on the well-being of the organization, or an organization acting to achieve its objectives in a way that ignores its impact on the well-being of the surrounding sector or community or environment. Horizontal facilitation favors power denying love because it prioritizes the self-realization of individual group members over the unity of the group. (This statement follows from the definitions I have used, even though it sounds surprising because of the common oppressive connotation of the word *power*.)

Second, love, when exercised in a way that denies agency and power (the whole ignoring the constituent parts), becomes degenerative falling-down love (love that saps power and leaves the lover unable to stand up). In a couple, for example, love denying power is manifested by the person who is so focused on the growth and well-being of the partnership that they neglect their partner's and especially their own growth and well-being (as in love songs that say, "I can't live without you"). In a company, it is layoffs to prevent bankruptcy. Vertical facilitation favors love denying power because it prioritizes the self-realization and unity of the group over the self-realization of individual group members. (This also sounds surprising because of the common romantic connotation of the word *love*.) In these examples, degenerative love employs power-over to enforce the primacy of the whole ("I am hurting you for the larger good").

And third, it is only when power and love are exercised together that they become generative power-with and lifting-up love. In a couple, it is becoming more fully one as a partnership that is realizing itself and at the same time becoming more fully two as individuals who are both realizing themselves. In an organization, it is the balancing of the good of smaller wholes (employees), the larger whole (the organization), and even larger wholes (sector, community, environment). Such balancing is not straightforward.

Power and love exercised together produce transformative facilitation, where the self-realization of larger wholes and smaller constituent wholes is mutually reinforcing. There is no static point of balance between the poles of love and power: just like balancing the poles of verticality and horizontality, dynamic balancing involves moving back and forth, as we do in when we walk on two legs.

My broadened theory, then, was that facilitation can only be transformative if it employs both love and power. US civil rights leader Martin Luther King Jr., who had written his doctoral dissertation on Tillich's theology, expressed this imperative in his final presidential address to the Southern Christian Leadership Conference, eight months before he was assassinated:

Power properly understood is nothing but the ability to achieve purpose. It is the strength required to bring about

social, political, and economic change . . . And one of the
great problems of history is that the concepts of love and
power have usually been contrasted as opposites—polar
opposites—so that love is identified with the resignation
of power, and power with the denial of love . . . Now
we've got to get this thing right. What is needed is a realization that power without love is reckless and abusive,
and love without power is sentimental and anemic . . . It
is precisely this collision of immoral power with power-
less morality which constitutes the major crisis of our
time.[6]

For the facilitator to be able to help unblock power in the work
of a group, the facilitator has to be able to unblock it within themself. I have usually felt comfortable with the drive toward self-
realization: my experiences of privilege and masculinity have
supported this orientation. My drive toward self-realization has
served me well in developing and employing my gifts in the service of the groups I work with. My evolution as a facilitator has
been to learn to employ both my power and my love, not by weak-
ening my stronger drive (power), but by strengthening my
weaker one (love). A facilitator has to bring to the work both their
full contribution and their full connection, to be able to support
participants to do the same.

JUSTICE IS THE STRUCTURE THAT ENABLES
LOVE AND POWER

Even after *Power and Love* was published, I still had a nagging
sense that my theory was missing something crucial. When I sent
the draft manuscript to Arenas, she wrote back: "I see a certain
naïveté in your vision of a balance between power and love, in
which things can be improved leaving everyone satisfied. How
can that be? In a context of great imbalance or inequity, as in
Guatemala, how can poverty be uprooted without some sectors

of society (of power, of course) being very dissatisfied? It is their economic interests which will be affected. I think that balance and satisfaction for all are possible in the realm of discourse, but not when you go down to 'real' politics in a context of enormous inequality." And when I presented the book at a seminar in the Netherlands, Jeremy Baskin, a trade unionist and academic, observed that my theory lacked a teleology—that it didn't explain how social change processes are directed toward an objective or shaped by a purpose.

I thought that what I was missing might be related to justice; the Tillich book I had used as a reference is titled *Love, Power, and Justice.* But even though I came back many times to what Tillich and King had written about justice, and could see the centrality of the search for justice in many of my projects (starting with the Mont Fleur team's search for a way to effect the transition away from apartheid oppression), I couldn't make out what this meant for my theory of facilitation.

If you sit with a question for long enough, sometimes you discover that the answer was in front of you all along. In this case, I found a clue in mulling over another puzzling experience I had had, in Thailand in 2010. My colleagues and I were starting the project to deal with the ongoing political conflict between pro- and antigovernment forces that had produced violent clashes on the streets of Bangkok. The project organizers had set up a series of conversations for us with a range of stakeholder leaders—from politics, business, the military, the media, the aristocracy, civil society—and for three full days we sat in a bright windowless hotel meeting room and met with these leaders one after another.

At the time I was bewildered by this experience of listening to a series of strong-minded leaders giving their views of this complicated conflict in a context and culture that were unfamiliar to me. But later I realized that, at another level, what we had been hearing was simple: every single person had been trying to get us on their side by convincing us that they were right and their opponents were wrong—and more specifically, that they were being treated unfairly and were the victims of injustice. Moreover, every single person had come to the hotel to meet us because they thought that Thailand wasn't as good as it could or should be, and they wanted to contribute to making it better. Everyone was, from their own perspective, demanding justice.

I have come to understand that this aspiration for justice is a third universal drive that is required for the practice of transformative facilitation. In most collaborations, most participants assert that the system they are part of needs to become (among other things) more fair, respectful, inclusive, equitable, or just. Even though different people have radically different experiences of justice and injustice and different ways of thinking about these phenomena (often, as in Thailand, these ways of thinking are self-serving, that what is happening is that *I* am being treated unjustly), most of them appeal to justice as an important objective.

People typically assert the imperative of justice at two levels: as an end for their collaboration (a more just system that they are working together to create, in their organization, community, or society) and also as a means for their collaboration (a more just process for their working together). This assertion does not mean that justice, any more than love or power, is easy or straightforward to achieve—only that it is a broadly acknowledged imperative that, explicitly or implicitly, provides a direction or objective for collaboration.

This insight into the importance of the drive toward justice brought me back, once again, to Tillich's framework. He defines justice as "the form in which the power of being activates itself . . . and through which love performs its work."[7] In this sense, injustice occurs in structures and practices that are not simply unfair but in which the intrinsic claim of any being to realize itself (to live and grow) is rejected: when the power-to of some is allowed to suffocate the power-to of others. Two stark examples of such injustice are the US criminal justice system that enabled Minneapolis police officer Derek Chauvin to kneel on the neck of George Floyd, and the health system that during the pandemic produced higher mortality among marginalized people. In an organization, injustice is manifested in the written and unwritten rules that produce fewer opportunities for contribution and connection by women, minorities, and lower-rank employees.

Facilitation must therefore help participants harness not only love and power but also justice. In the Haitian, Mexican, Guatemalan, and Thai processes mentioned earlier, justice was both an objective and a principle for the work to address the problematic situations that were the reason these processes had been initiated. In everyday collaborations, justice is also both an objective and a form for the work to make particular problematic situations better. Justice is the practice of removing structural obstacles so as to enable the full employment of love and power toward a higher purpose.

For the facilitator to be able to help unblock justice in the work of a group, the facilitator has to be able to unblock it within themself. I understand that part of my responsibility as a facilitator is to help participants contribute and connect equitably. But my lifetime of privilege—my lack of a felt experience of injustice— means that I am sometimes oblivious to the ways in which injustice (sexism, racism, rankism, etc.) skew contribution and connection in the groups I'm working with. My colleagues have helped me notice more and act accordingly to, as Palestinian facilitator Zoughbi Zoughbi once put it to me, "afflict the comfortable and comfort the afflicted." A facilitator has to bring justice into their own practice to be able to support participants to do the same.

I've talked about the place of justice in our work with my colleague Rebecca Freeth, who has facilitated and participated in many processes dealing with racial issues in South Africa. She sees justice as "both about how we navigate our way through social change processes (being conscious of unequal degrees of privilege, seeking parity of participation, and being willing to engage with our own outrage and that of others) and the direction in which we point our social change efforts (toward greater justice)."[8]

Justice provides critical guidance for both the means and the ends of collaboration. Without a drive toward justice, collaboration can, as Arenas warned me, merely reproduce an unjust status quo. Justice enables collaboration to transcend and break through such compromise and stuckness.

In the King speech I quoted earlier, he went on to say, "Power at its best is love implementing the demands of justice, and justice at its best is power correcting everything that stands against love."[9] King thought that love, power, and justice were all required to realize social transformation. I think that all three are required to realize the potential of transformative facilitation.

King also asserted that "the arc of the moral universe is long, but it bends towards justice."[10] Transformative facilitation helps participants and facilitators work together with greater awareness of and responsibility for their roles in what is happening among themselves and in the larger system. It therefore offers an opportunity to contribute to bending the moral universe toward justice.

Transformative facilitation offers a larger possibility

When I am paying attention to what is happening in a group, I am observing both the specific details in front of me and also the larger patterns of love, power, and justice and how these are enabling or disabling the group's progress. Similarly, when I pay attention to the practice of transformative facilitation in different contexts around the world, I observe both its contribution to helping these groups transform their specific problematic situations and also its larger potential as a way for people to transform the systems that are producing and reproducing disconnection, disempowerment, and injustice.

Most of the groups I work with are trying, with passionate commitment, in their own spheres, large or small, to create a world with more love, power, and justice. They know that forcing won't work and so they are trying to help people move forward together.

Some of these groups succeed and some do not. This body of work demonstrates that it *is* possible to collaborate and make progress: it is not straightforward or easy or guaranteed, but it can be done.

Transformative facilitation enables progress by removing the obstacles to love, power, and justice. In November 2020, as I was finishing this book, I spoke again with Francisco de Roux, the Colombian priest whose observation three years earlier, that I was "removing the obstacles to the expression of the mystery," had inspired me to begin it. During these three years, de Roux had been president of the Commission for the Clarification of Truth, Coexistence, and Non-Repetition, trying, amid continuing polarization and demonization, to help Colombians move forward together. In this conversation, he sounded exhausted from having organized so many meetings among so many diverse people and yet struggling to make progress. "There is no future without opening up to one another, with sincerity, as fellow human beings," he said. "There is no other formula."

It is only through opening up to one another that we can enable love, power, and justice. And it is only through working with love, power, and justice that we can move forward together. There is no other formula for creating a better world.

A Map of Transformative Facilitation

*I*n chapters 3–10, I explained that the practice of transformative facilitation involves making five pairs of outer moves, enabled by five inner shifts, as and when these are needed, moment by moment, to help a group move forward together. The map provided on the following pages summarizes this whole practice.

The table shows, overall and for each of the five basic collaboration questions, the typical answers, upsides, and downsides of vertical facilitation (the three left-hand columns) and of horizontal facilitation (the three right-hand columns). It also shows (in the central three columns) the moves and shifts employed in transformative facilitation to cycle between the vertical and horizontal.

The order of the columns illustrates the following key points about the practice of transformative facilitation. The facilitator uses the ten moves to help the group get the best of the upsides of vertical and horizontal facilitation and avoid the worst of the downsides. As in the figure in chapter 3, the facilitator does this by cycling between the five pairs of countervailing moves: when the group is dipping into the downside of one pole, the facilitator makes the move that encourages the group to move toward the upside of the opposite pole.

The facilitator is able to cycle fluidly between these pairs of outer moves through making five inner shifts. In working with the first question, "How do we see our situation?" for example, the facilitator employs and encourages inquiring to avoid the downsides (groupthink and repudiation) of the vertical "We have the right answer," and employs and encourages advocating to

Table M.1: A Map of Transformative Facilitation

COLLABORATION QUESTION	VERTICAL FACILITATION			Outer move toward the horizontal
	Typical answer	*Downsides*	*Upsides*	
Overall	"We must focus on the singular good of the whole"	Rigidity and domination	Coordination and coherence	Emphasizing plurality
1. How do we see our situation?	"We have the right answer"	Groupthink and repudiation	Expertise and decisiveness	Inquiring
2. How do we define success?	"We need to agree"	Unachievability and insufficiency	A finish line	Advancing
3. How do we get from here to there?	"We know the way"	Dead end and over a cliff	A clear route	Discovering
4. How do we decide who does what?	"Our leaders decide"	Subordination and insubordination	Authority and alignment	Accompanying
5. How do we understand our role?	"We must fix this"	Coldness and abdication	Objectivity	Standing inside

	TRANSFORMATIVE FACILITATION	HORIZONTAL FACILITATION		
Inner shift	Outer move toward the vertical	Upsides	Downsides	Typical answer
Attending	Emphasizing unity	Autonomy and variety	Fragmentation and gridlock	"We must focus on the good of each part"
Opening	Advocating	Diversity and inclusion	Cacophony and indecision	"We each have our own answer"
Discerning	Concluding	Pragmatism	Insubstantiality and dispersion	"We each need to keep moving"
Adapting	Mapping	Flexibility	Divergence and disorganization	"We will each find our way as we go"
Serving	Directing	Self-motivated actions	Separateness and misalignment	"We each decide for ourselves"
Partnering	Standing outside	Self-responsibility	Myopia	"We must each put our own house in order"

avoid the downsides (cacophony and indecision) of the horizontal "We each have our own answer." The facilitator is able to cycle between inquiring and advocating through opening.

In summary, the table emphasizes that, through making these moves and shifts, the facilitator helps the group stay mostly on the middle path of the upsides (the darkly shaded area) and not to stray too far or for too long into the peripheral downsides (the lightly shaded areas).

Notes

Foreword

1. Ed Schein and Warren Bennis, *Personal and Organizational Change through Group Methods: The Laboratory Approach* (New York: Wiley, 1965); Don Michael, *Learning to Plan and Planning to Learn* (Alexandria, VA: Miles River Press, 1987).

2. Ed Schein, *Process Consultation: Its Role in Organization Development* (Reading, MA: Addison-Wesley, 1969); Peter Senge, *The Fifth Discipline: The Art and Practice of the Learning Organization* (New York: Doubleday, 2006); Ronald Heifetz, *Leadership without Easy Answers* (Cambridge, MA: Belknap, 1994); Otto Scharmer, *Theory U: Leading from the Future as It Emerges* (Oakland, CA: Berrett-Koehler, 2009); and Gervase Bushe and Robert Marshak, eds., *Dialogic Organization Development* (Oakland, CA: Berrett-Koehler, 2015).

Preface

1. Kurt Lewin, "Problems of Research in Social Psychology," in *Field Theory in Social Science: Selected Theoretical Papers*, ed. D. Cartwright, (New York: Harper & Row, 1951), 169.

Introduction: "You Are Removing the Obstacles to the Expression of the Mystery!"

1. These methodologies are described in Adam Kahane, *Transformative Scenario Planning: Working Together to Change the Future* (Oakland, CA: Berrett-Koehler, 2012); David Cooperrider and Diana Whitney, *Appreciative Inquiry: A Positive Revolution in Change* (Oakland, CA: Berrett-Koehler, 2005); adrienne maree brown, *Emergent Strategy: Shaping Change, Changing Worlds* (Chico, CA: AK Press, 2017); Marvin Weisbord and Sandra Janoff, *Future Search: An Action Guide to Finding Common Ground in Organizations and*

Communities (Oakland, CA: Berrett-Koehler, 2010); Harrison Owen, *Open Space Technology: A User's Guide*, 3rd edition (Oakland, CA: Berrett-Koehler, 2008); Zaid Hassan, *The Social Labs Revolution: A New Approach to Solving Our Most Complex Challenges* (Oakland, CA: Berrett-Koehler, 2014); and Otto Scharmer, *Theory U: Leading from the Future as It Emerges* (Oakland, CA: Berrett-Koehler, 2009).

2. See, for example, Marianne Mille Bojer, Heiko Roehl, Marianne Knuth, and Colleen Magner, *Mapping Dialogue: Essential Tools for Social Change* (Chagrin Falls, OH: Taos Institute, 2008); John Heron, *The Complete Facilitator's Handbook* (Seattle: Kogan Page, 1999); Peggy Holman, Tom Devane, and Steven Cady, eds., *The Change Handbook: Group Methods for Shaping the Future* (Oakland, CA: Berrett-Koehler, 2007); Sam Kaner, *Facilitator's Guide to Participatory Decision-Making* (San Francisco: Jossey-Bass, 2014); Henri Lipmanowicz and Keith McCandless, *The Surprising Power of Liberating Structures* (Seattle: Liberating Structures Press, 2014); Roger Schwarz, *The Skilled Facilitator: A Comprehensive Resource for Consultants, Facilitators, Coaches, and Trainers* (San Francisco: Jossey-Bass, 2016); and Brian Stanfield, *The Workshop Book: From Individual Creativity to Group Action* (Gabriola Island, British Columbia: New Society, 2002).

CHAPTER 3: Unconventional Transformative Facilitation Breaks through Constraints

1. This model for understanding and working with polarities is based on Barry Johnson's body of theory and practice, summarized in his books *Polarity Management: Identifying and Managing Unsolvable Problems* (Amherst, MA: Human Resource Development Press, 2014) and *And: Making a Difference by Leveraging Polarity, Paradox or Dilemma* (Amherst, MA: Human Resource Development Press, 2020).

2. Gilmore Crosby, *Planned Change: Why Kurt Lewin's Social Science Is Still Best Practice for Business Results, Change Management, and Human Progress* (New York: Productivity Press, 2020), 8–9. Crosby quotes Kurt Lewin, *Group Decision and Social Change* (New York: Henry Holt, 1948), 280.

CHAPTER 5: The Facilitator Knows What Move to Make
Next by Paying Attention

1. Quote from the website www.theinnergame.com. See also
   Timothy Gallwey, *The Inner Game of Tennis: The Classic Guide to
   the Mental Side of Peak Performance* (New York: Random House,
   1997).

2. John Geirland, "Go with the Flow," *Wired*, Issue 4.09
   (September 1996), https://www.wired.com/1996/09/czik/.

3. Otto Scharmer, *Theory U: Leading from the Future as It Emerges*
   (Oakland, CA: Berrett-Koehler, 2009).

4. Adin Steinsaltz, *Koren Talmud Bavli* (Jerusalem: Koren Publishers,
   2012). Quoted in https://steinsaltz.org/daf/shabbat31/.

CHAPTER 6: How Do We See Our Situation?

1. See Adam Kahane, *Transformative Scenario Planning: Working
   Together to Change the Future* (Oakland, CA: Berrett-Koehler,
   2012), 1–13.

2. Shunryu Suzuki, *Zen Mind, Beginner's Mind* (Boston: Shambhala,
   2011), 1.

3. Edgar Schein, *Humble Consulting: How to Provide Real Help Faster*
   (Oakland, CA: Berrett-Koehler, 2016), xi.

4. Schein, *Humble Consulting*, xiv, 171.

5. Peter Senge, *The Fifth Discipline: The Art and Practice of the Learning
   Organization* (New York: Doubleday, 2006), 183.

6. See Bryan Smith, "Building Shared Vision: How to Begin" and Louis
   van der Merwe, "Bringing Diverse People to Common Purpose," in
   Peter Senge, ed., *The Fifth Discipline Fieldbook: Strategies and Tools
   for Building a Learning Organization* (New York: Currency, 1994),
   312, 424.

7. Kees van der Heijden, *Scenarios: The Art of Strategic Conversation*
   (Chichester, United Kingdom: Wiley, 1996).

8. Adapted from Otto Scharmer, *Theory U: Leading from the Future as
   It Emerges* (Oakland: Berrett-Koehler, 2009).

9. See Per Kristiansen and Robert Rasmussen, *Building a Better Business Using the Lego Serious Play Method* (Chichester, United Kingdom: Wiley, 2014).

10. Carl Rogers, "A Theory of Therapy, Personality, and Interpersonal Relationships, as Developed in the Client-Centered Framework," in *Psychology: A Study of a Science,* vol. 3, ed. Sigmund Koch (New York, NY: McGraw-Hill, 1959), 209.

CHAPTER 7: How Do We Define Success?

1. See Susan Sweitzer, "Sustainable Food Lab Learning History Chapter 2," https://www.scribd.com/document/26436901/SFL-LH -Chapter-2-Public, 12, and the project website: sustainablefoodlab.org.

2. See Adam Kahane, *Transformative Scenario Planning: Working Together to Change the Future* (Oakland: Berrett-Koehler, 2012), 79–90.

3. "Siempre en búsqueda de la paz" ["Always Searching for Peace"], October 7, 2016, es.presidencia.gov.co.

4. John Gottman and Nan Silver, *The Seven Principles for Making Marriage Work: A Practical Guide from the Country's Foremost Relationship Expert* (New York: Harmony, 2015), 129–130.

5. Organization of American States, *Scenarios for the Drug Problem in the Americas 2013–2025* (Washington, DC: Author, 2013).

6. José Miguel Insulza, "The OAS Drug Report: 16 Months of Debates and Consensus" (Washington, DC: Organization of American States, 2014).

7. John Keats, *The Complete Poetical Works and Letters of John Keats* (Boston: Houghton, Mifflin, 1899), 277.

CHAPTER 8: How Do We Get from Here to There?

1. Mike Berardino, "Mike Tyson Explains One of His Most Famous Quotes," *South Florida Sun Sentinel,* November 9, 2012. https://www .sun-sentinel.com/sports/fl-xpm-2012-11-09-sfl-mike-tyson-explains -one-of-his-most-famous-quotes-20121109-story.html.

2. Antonio Machado, "Caminante, no hay camino, se hace camino al andar," in "Proverbios y cantares XXIX," *Campos de Castilla* (Madrid: Editorial Poesia eres tu, 2006), 131.

3. Adam Kahane, "What *Avengers: Infinity War* Can Teach Us about Business," *strategy+business*, 98, December 10, 2019/Spring 2020. https://www.strategy-business.com/blog/What-Avengers-Infinity -War-can-teach-us-about-business?gko=d0b4b.

4. Dwight Eisenhower, *The Papers of Dwight David Eisenhower*, ed. Louis Galambos (Baltimore: Johns Hopkins University Press, 1984), 1516.

5. *The Mystery of Picasso*, written and directed by Henri-Georges Clouzot, film (1956; Paris: Filmsonor).

6. Glennifer Gillespie, "The Footprints of Mont Fleur: The Mont Fleur Scenario Project, South Africa, 1991–1992," in *Learning Histories: Democratic Dialogue Regional Project*, ed. Katrin Käufer. (New York: United Nations Development Programme Regional Bureau for Latin America and the Caribbean, 2004). http://reospartners.com/wp -content/uploads/old/Mont%20Fleur%20Learning%20History.pdf?

7. The pioneering text he recommended to me was Michael Doyle and David Straus, *How to Make Meetings Work!* (New York: Berkley, 1993). See also David Chrislip, *The Collaborative Leadership Fieldbook* (San Francisco: Jossey-Bass, 2002).

8. Henry Mintzberg, "Crafting Strategy," *Harvard Business Review*, July 1987. https://hbr.org/1987/07/crafting-strategy.

CHAPTER 9: How Do We Decide Who Does What?

1. William J. O'Brien, *Character at Work: Building Prosperity through the Practice of Virtue* (Boston: Paulist Press, 2008), viii.

CHAPTER 10: How Do We Understand Our Role?

1. Melanie MacKinnon et al., *Wahbung: Our Tomorrows Imagined* (Winnipeg: Assembly of Manitoba Chiefs, 2019), https://manito bachiefs.com/wp-content/uploads/Wahbung-Web-1-copy.Nov5_.pdf.

2. See Melanie MacKinnon and Adam Kahane, "Braiding Indigenous and Settler Methodologies: Learnings from a First Nations Health Transformation Project in Manitoba," Reos blog, December 13, 2019. https://reospartners.com/braiding-indigenous-and-settler -methodologies-learnings-from-a-first-nations-health-transformation -project-in-manitoba/.

3. Audre Lorde, "The Master's Tools Will Never Dismantle the Master's House," in *Sister Outsider: Essays and Speeches* (Berkeley, CA: Crossing Press, 2007), 110–114.

4. Ronald Heifetz and Marty Linsky, "A Survival Guide for Leaders," *Harvard Business Review*, June 2002. https://hbr.org/2002/06/a -survival-guide-for-leaders

5. Robert Johnson, *Owning Your Own Shadow: Understanding the Dark Side of the Psyche* (New York: Harper One, 1993), 89.

Conclusion: Removing the Obstacles to Love, Power, and Justice

1. See Adam Kahane, *Power and Love: A Theory and Practice of Social Change* (Oakland, CA: Berrett-Koehler, 2009).

2. See Adam Kahane, *Solving Tough Problems: An Open Way of Talking, Listening, and Creating New Realities* (Oakland, CA: Berrett-Koehler, 2004), 113–122.

3. Elena Díez Pinto, "Building Bridges of Trust: Visión Guatemala, 1998–2000," in *Learning Histories: Democratic Dialogue Regional Project*, ed. Katrin Käufer. (New York: United Nations Development Programme Regional Bureau for Latin America and the Caribbean, 2004).

4. Paul Tillich, *Love, Power, and Justice: Ontological Analyses and Ethical Applications* (New York: Oxford University Press, 1954), 25.

5. Tillich, *Love, Power, and Justice*, 36.

6. Martin Luther King Jr., "Where Do We Go from Here?" in *The Essential Martin Luther King, Jr.*, ed. Clayborne Carson (Boston: Beacon Press, 2013), 220–221. Carson is the founding director of the Martin Luther King Jr. Research and Education Institute at Stanford University.

7. Tillich, *Love, Power, and Justice*, 56, 71.

8. LeAnne Grillo, "Power, Love, and Justice: An Interview of Rebecca Freeth," Reos blog, https://reospartners.com/power-love-and-justice -an-interview-with-rebecca-freeth/2012.

9. King, "Where Do We Go?" 221. Other published versions of this speech give this phrase as "Justice at its best is love correcting everything that stands against love," which I think makes less sense.

10. Martin Luther King Jr., "Out of the Long Night," in *The Gospel Messenger* (Elgin, IL: Church of the Brethren, 1958), 3.

Acknowledgments

I am enormously grateful for the support and kindness of many colleagues, friends, and family, without whom I would not have been able to write this book.

Facilitation is a team sport, and this book distills what I have learned from playing on many wonderful facilitation teams, including with Negusu Aklilu, Marcia Anderson, Antonio Aranibar, Steve Atkinson, Brenna Atnikov, Jeff Barnum, Veronica Baz, Adam Blackwell, Dinesh Budhram, Mille Bøjer, Stina Brown, Manuel José Carvajal, Sumit Champrasit, David Chrislip, Charles Clermont, Moriah Davis, Elena Díez Pinto, Jean Paul Faubert, Betty Sue Flowers, Rebecca Freeth, Rossana Fuentes, Leigh Gassner, Mesfin Getachew, Melanie Goodchild, LeAnne Grillo, Hal Hamilton, Avner Haramati, Zaid Hassan, Joseph Jaworski, Tejaswinee Jhunjhunwala, Dorothy Kahane, Mike Kang, Goft Kanyaporn, Maianne Knuth, Pieter le Roux, Anaí Linares, Aeumporn Loipradit, Melanie MacKinnon, Julio Madrazo, Arun Maira, Vincent Maphai, Gerardo Marquez, Luis René Martínez, Joe McCarron, Grady McGonagill, Jacquie McLemore, Amanda Meawasige, Joaquin Moreno, Lerato Mpofu, Gustavo Mutis, Choice Ndoro, Bill O'Brien, Wendy Palmer, Dean Parisian, Reola Phelps, Elizabeth Pinnington, Monica Pohlmann, Ian Prinsloo, Manuela Restrepo, Otto Scharmer, Christel Scholten, Paul Simons, Wondwossen Sintayehu, Fah Snidwongse, Darlene Spence, Jorge Talavera, Kees van der Heijden, Louis van der Merwe, and David Winter.

I have been able to do this challenging work because I am part of the strong Reos Partners team, including Steve Atkinson, Brenna Atnikov, Mille Bøjer, Jennifer Falb, Jessica Fan, Rebecca

Freeth, LeAnne Grillo, Tejaswinee Jhunjhunwala, Mike Kang, Colleen Korniak, Colleen Magner, Gerardo Marquez, Jacquie McLemore, Josephine Pallandt, Monica Pohlmann, Ian Prinsloo, Manuela Restrepo, Christel Scholten, Mariaan Smith, Mahmood Sonday, and David Winter. I especially appreciate the steadfast support of my longtime business partner Joe McCarron.

I have received generous feedback on drafts of this book from Andrew Akpan, Marcia Anderson, Sean Andrew, David Archer, Clara Arenas, Robin Athey, John Atkinson, Brenna Atnikov, Rich Ann Baetz, Phoebe Barnard, Dorian Baroni, Jany Barraut, Nik Beeson, Blanka Bellak, Stefan Bergheim, Marcia Bevilaqua, Peter Block, Mille Bøjer, Simon Bold, Stacy Boss, Jean-Paul Bourque, Freya Bradford, Sarah Brooks, Santiago Campos, Miguel Canas, Stephen Carman, Manuel José Carvajal, Bernadette Castilho, Mandy Cavanaugh, Ankit Chhabra, Aman Chitkara, David Chrislip, Elizabeth Clement, Charles Clermont, Laure Cohen, Val Porter Cook, Mithymna Corke, Chris Corrigan, Josefina Coutiño, Allia DeAngelis, Nele De Peuter, Ciska De Pillecyn, Keita Demming, Umesh Dhand, Rebecca Downie, Scott Drimie, Amy Emmert, Emile Enongene, Josh Epperson, Thomas Everill, Russell Fisher, Betty Sue Flowers, Gwynne Foster, Gerarda Frederick, Mike Freedman, Arti Freeman, Rebecca Freeth, Hermann Funk, Mesfin Getachew, Jim Gimian, Cathy Glover, Ernest Godin, George Goens, Pierre Goirand, Carol Gorelick, Paul Hackenmueller, Saleena Ham, Calvin Haney, Toby Harper-Merrett, Lynn Harris, Chip Hauss, Geoff Hazell, Meghan Hellstern, Kira Higgs, Daniel Hirschler, Ard Hordijk, Vincent Hudson, Constantine Iliopoulos, Jake Jacobs, Cedric Jamet, Rachel Jones, Rose Kattackal, Ruhiye Keskin, Art Kleiner, Christian Koehler, Susan Kolodin, Ruth Krivoy, Pascal Kruijsifix, Sylvie Kwayeb, Elizabeth Lancaster, Richard Lent, Tom Lent, Cedric Levitre, Stephanie Levy, Kathy Lewis, Lisa Lim-Cole, Victor Loh, Bill Mcallister Lovatt, Jon Lukin, Melanie MacKinnon, Pedro Magalh, Maria Grazia Magazzino, Gerardo Marquez, Nadine McCormick, Joseph McIntyre, Hyun-Duck McKay, Claire McKendrick, Pauline Melnyk, Parand

Meysami, Kath Milne, Maria Montejo, Jerry Nagel, Jo Nelson, Maria Ana Neves, Tara Polzer Ngwato, Sibout Nooteboom, Riichiro Oda, Seamus O'Gorman, Johannus Olsthoorn, Caroline Pakel, Josephine Pallandt, Mikael Paltschik, Manuela Petersen, Roger Peterson, Steve Piersanti, Monica Pohlmann, Monica Porteanu, Ian Prinsloo, Antares Reisky, Caroline Rennie, Manuela Restrepo, Marc Rettig, Sean Roark, Alison Roper, Michael Rozyne, Catherine Sands, Jorge Sanint, Iina Santamäki, Stefano Savi, Ed Schein, Peter Schein, Silva Sedrakian, Henry Senko, Mark Silberg, Candace Sinclair, Arjun Singh, Navjeet Singh, Liz Skelton, Gustav Sørensen, Antonio Starnino, Ilka Stein, Ramona-Denisa Steiper, Bob Stilger, Daniel Stillman, Di Strachan, Nicol Suhr, Doug Sundheim, Andrea Swanson, Jill Swenson, Anouk Talen, Svenja Tams, Terrence Taylor, Chris Thompson, Greg Thorson, Marco Valente, Louis van der Merwe, Pascal Wattiaux, Doug Weinfield, Ian Wight, David Winter, Teresa Woodland, and Joel Yanowitz.

I have been able to write and publish this and my previous books because of my partnership with the excellent team at Berrett-Koehler, including Susan Geraghty, Daniel Tesser, Michele D. Jones, Cathy Mallon, Carolyn Thibault, Maria Jesus Aguilo, Shabnam Banerjee-McFarland, Valerie Caldwell, Leslie Crandell, Michael Crowley, Sohayla Farman, Kristen Frantz, Catherine Lengronne, Zoe Mackey, Katie Sheehan, and Jeevan Sivasubramaniam. I especially value the brilliant support of my extraordinary editor, Steve Piersanti.

Finally, I am buoyed up by the love of my family, including Allan, Olivia, Alexander, and James Boesak; Lieneke and Shane Dennis; Bernard, David, Jed, and Naomi Kahane; Caelin, Daniel, and Joshua Thyssen; Belen, Jean Pierre, Siobhan, and Ciaran Wilkinson; Pulane, Apollo, Zion, Marley, and Sinai Zake; and especially Dorothy, who enabled everything.

Index

Page numbers in italics denote illustrative material.

About the Author

*A*dam Kahane has spent more than thirty years facilitating breakthrough.

Adam is a director of Reos Partners, an international social enterprise that helps people work together to address their most important and intractable issues.

Adam has facilitated leadership teams of companies, governments, foundations, churches, educational institutions, political parties, and nonprofit organizations. He has also facilitated diverse teams of leaders from across larger social systems at the local, state, national, and global levels, including executives and politicians, generals and guerrillas, civil servants and trade unionists, artists and activists. He has facilitated a variety of collaborative processes, some over hours or days and others over months or years.

He has done this work in more than fifty countries, all around the world.

Adam has helped groups work together on all kinds of external and internal challenges facing their organizations. He has also helped cross-organizational groups work together on many of the most critical challenges of our time: climate change, racial equity, democratic governance, Indigenous rights, health, food, energy, water, education, justice, and security. He has helped people bridge divides in, among other places, the US, Canada, Colombia, Haiti, Northern Ireland, Israel, Zimbabwe, Ethiopia, Myanmar, and Thailand.

Before cofounding Reos Partners, Adam was head of global social, political, economic, environmental, and technological scenarios at Shell in London. He has held research positions at universities and institutes in North America, Europe, Japan, and South Africa, including as an associate fellow at the Saïd School of Business at the University of Oxford.

Adam is the author of four best-selling books: *Solving Tough Problems: An Open Way of Talking, Listening, and Creating New Realities* (which Nelson Mandela called "a breakthrough book that addresses the central challenge of our time: finding a way to work together to solve the problems we have created"); *Power and Love: A Theory and Practice of Social Change*; *Transformative Scenario Planning: Working Together to Change the Future*; and *Collaborating with the Enemy: How to Work with People You Don't Agree with or Like or Trust*.

Adam has an BSc in physics from McGill University; an MA in energy and resources from the University of California, Berkeley; and an MA in applied behavioral science from Bastyr University.

Adam and his wife, Dorothy, have four children and ten grandchildren. They live in Montreal and Cape Town.

www.adamkahane.com

About Reos Partners

HOW CAN WE WORK TOGETHER TO SOLVE THE PROBLEMS WE HAVE CREATED?

Reos Partners is an international social enterprise that knows how to make real progress.

We've been designing and facilitating systemic change projects for more than twenty years and have built up a rigorous set of transformative methods for addressing complex, stuck challenges.

Using a pragmatic and creative approach, we partner with governments, corporations, and civil society organizations on humanity's most crucial issues: education, health, food, energy, the environment, development, justice, security, and peace. Again and again, we enable people mired in complexity, confusion, and conflict to work together to construct new realities—and a better future.

WE HELP YOU CHALLENGE THE STATUS QUO, TOGETHER

The starting point for progress is a diverse coalition that is ready to challenge the status quo. Every Reos Partners project brings together participants from across a whole system: politicians, activists, executives, generals, guerrillas, unionists, activists, artists, researchers, clergy, community leaders, and others. Diversity may feel like the problem, but it is at the heart of problem solving. Working as guides, we skillfully engage people with different perspectives and interests to collaborate on shared concerns.

Proven methods for systemic change

Reos Partners projects occur at three scales: events of a few days, processes of several months, and platforms that operate for years. A single event can spark new insights, relationships, and capacities; a long-term platform can enable new experiments, initiatives, and movements—and, ultimately, systemic transformation.

We take a custom approach to every situation, but we often employ a combination of two tested approaches: transformative scenarios processes and social labs. We also offer training and coaching to build the capacities and skills that enable enduring systems change.

Real progress on vital challenges, worldwide

We've learned that there is no quick fix: systemic change takes time, energy, resources, and skill. But with these in place, our most successful projects take on lives of their own, spawning resilient networks, alliances, and ecologies.

Let's work together

We operate both globally and locally, with offices in Cambridge (Massachusetts), Geneva, Johannesburg, London, Melbourne, Montreal, and São Paulo.

ReosPartners

www.reospartners.com

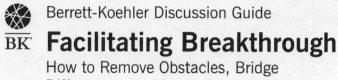

Berrett-Koehler Discussion Guide

BK Facilitating Breakthrough

How to Remove Obstacles, Bridge
Differences, and Move Forward Together

The Theory of Transformative Facilitation

Transformative facilitation is a powerful approach to helping a group
of people collaborate to transform their situation. The following discussion questions can help you assess the value of this approach in
your situation:

- What is the situation you are facing? Do you see this situation as
  problematic (you want it to change), and if so, in what respect?
  Who else sees this situation as problematic and in what respects?

- How do you want to deal with this situation: By forcing it to be
  the way you want it to be? By adapting to it as it is? By exiting the
  situation? By collaborating with others to change it? How do other
  people who see the situation as problematic want to deal with it?

- If you want to collaborate to change your situation, with whom do
  you need to collaborate to be able to effect change? How could you
  enroll these people in a collaboration?

- Whom do you want to act as a facilitator to help this group of collaborators move forward together? Yourself? Another member of the
  group? Someone from outside the group? Several of you together?

- What approach to facilitation are you and the group accustomed
  to using? Is it vertical (focused on the good of the singular whole of
  the group), horizontal (focused on the good of each participant in
  the group), or transformative (focused on the good of the system of
  wholes and parts)? What have you experienced as the upsides and
  downsides of your approach?

- How does or could your group work with the following basic collaboration questions: How do we see our situation? How do we

define success? How will we get from here to there? How do we
decide who does what? How do we understand our role?

• What is your highest hope for your collaboration? Your worst fear?

The Practice of Transformative Facilitation

The core of the practice of transformative facilitation is making five
pairs of moves to help a group move forward together:

1. Advocating and inquiring
2. Concluding and advancing
3. Mapping and discovering
4. Directing and accompanying
5. Standing outside and standing inside

To do this, the facilitator needs to learn to use all of these moves
fluently and fluidly—and not to choose or favor only the vertical or
horizontal move in each pair. The following discussion questions can
help you increase your fluency with each of these moves:

• What signals tell you that you need to make this move?

• Based on your own experience of working with others (at work, at
home, in community), what is the positive contribution or upside of
making this move?

• What is the danger or downside of making this move?

• What are examples of ways you could make this move? In what settings could you practice?

• Which one of the pair do you tend to use more often? Which do you
tend to use when you are under stress? What holds you back from
using the other one more?

A facilitator moves fluidly among these ten outer moves by paying attention, and in particular by making five inner shifts:

1. Opening
2. Discerning
3. Adapting
4. Serving
5. Partnering

The following questions can help you improve your fluency with these shifts:

• What signals tell you that you need to make this shift?

• Based on your own experience of working with others, what is the value of making this shift? What do you hope will happen?

• What is the risk of making this shift? What do you fear will happen?

• What are examples of ways you could make this shift? In what settings could you practice?

Dear reader,

Thank you for picking up this book and welcome to the worldwide BK community! You're joining a special group of people who have come together to create positive change in their lives, organizations, and communities.

What's BK all about?

Our mission is to connect people and ideas to create a world that works for all.

Why? Our communities, organizations, and lives get bogged down by old paradigms of self-interest, exclusion, hierarchy, and privilege. But we believe that can change. That's why we seek the leading experts on these challenges—and share their actionable ideas with you.

A welcome gift

To help you get started, we'd like to offer you a **free copy** of one of our bestselling ebooks:

www.bkconnection.com/welcome

When you claim your **free ebook**, you'll also be subscribed to our blog.

Our freshest insights

Access the best new tools and ideas for leaders at all levels on our blog at ideas.bkconnection.com.

Sincerely,

Your friends at Berrett-Koehler